God's Man of™
Influence

JIM GEORGE

HARVEST HOUSE™ PUBLISHERS

EUGENE, OREGON

GOD'S MAN OF™ INFLUENCE
Copyright © 2003 by Jim George
Published by Harvest House Publishers
Eugene, Oregon 97402
www.harvesthousepublishers.com

Library of Congress Cataloging-in-Publication Data

George, Jim, 1943-
  God's man of influence / Jim George.
    p. cm.
Includes bibliographical references.
  ISBN 0-7369-1146-4 (pbk.)
  1. Christian men—Religious life. 2.   Influence (Psychology)—Religious aspects—Christianity.
I. Title.
BV4528.2.G455 2003
248.8'42—dc21   2003001909

Contents

A Word of Welcome

What does a man of influence look like and what does he do? What makes his life a life of lasting impact?

For the past 30 years, as I have sought to become a man of influence, I have studied the character of the men of influence God has placed in my life. I have also searched the Scriptures to glean an understanding of the traits of the godly men of the Bible.

What a joy it has been this past year to completely immerse myself in the study of influence—more specifically, the kind of influence that makes a lasting impact. For instance,

> Influence is a process.
>
> Influence is costly.
>
> Influence is never neutral.
>
> Influence is powerful.
>
> Influence is about people.
>
> Influence is demanding.
>
> Influence is hard won.
>
> Influence is easily lost.
>
> Influence is to be desired.
>
> Influence is everyone's privilege.
>
> Influence is everyone's responsibility.
>
> Influence is affected by relationships.
>
> Influence is attainable by anyone.

I am especially glad that you, too, desire to become a man who lives a life of lasting impact, and I look forward to our journey together toward becoming men of influence. Join with me as we take a profiling journey through the lives of a handful of history's greatest men of influence from the Bible. Join with me as we learn how our secret life of growth and maturity prepares us to have a public life of influence. Join with me as we inspect the outward signs of a man of influence. And, if you want to journey with me a little further, you will enjoy the application questions at the back of this book.

May God encourage and strengthen you as you make the journey of your life—the journey of becoming a man of influence.

Your fellow traveler,
Jim George

Part 1:

THE SECRETS OF A
LIFE OF INFLUENCE

My life shall touch a dozen lives
before this day is done,
Leave countless marks for good or ill
ere sets the evening sun.
This is the wish I always wish,
the prayer I always pray:
Lord, may my life help other lives
it touches by the way.[1]

PROFILING A MAN OF INFLUENCE

With God all things are possible.
—MATTHEW 19:26

In his 1955 Pulitzer Prize-winning book *Profiles in Courage,* the late president of the United States John F. Kennedy chronicled the life and stories of eight U.S. senators. He described and outlined how these men endured the pressures of public office—the risks to their careers, popularity with the people, defamation of their characters—all with great courage.

That book had a great impact on many in the 1960s generation and beyond. Kennedy was a profiler—he profiled the elements that demonstrated the courage of these political figures.[2] His book gave readers a better understanding of the lives and struggles of these eight senators.

Despite any "bad press," profiling can be a beneficial exercise. In my dictionary, *profiling* is defined as developing a list of characteristics that represent some one or some thing. This means that others can look at another person's life and develop a list of characteristics, such as his or her habits, principles, beliefs, and views. This list would then represent that person's life, becoming his or her profile.

The Profile of Your Life

Every person has a profile. Each person's profile—his or her patterns, habits, principles, and beliefs—indicates who he or she is as an individual. For instance, as a jogger, I have a specific profile. If you were to look at my life as a jogger you would see that I fit into a certain category of athletic endeavor and health. My professional status of pastor, writer, speaker, and teacher also gives me a certain profile. In fact, every profession and area of work has a specific profile.

Have you ever thought about your personal profile and whether your life will have a lasting impact? If people took a long look at your life, what would they see? Then, if they published their "research," what characteristics would they report by the patterns of your life? What qualities and habits would be evident for all to witness? In what ways are you influencing the lives of others?

I confess I'm not always pleased with the profile of my life! And the same is probably true of how you feel about your habits and activities, too. This is because, no matter what our profile, there is always room to grow. But one of the best ways for us to evaluate our own level of influence and possibly make some changes (hopefully for the better) is to look at the lives and profiles of others whose lives are worthy of copying.

So, together, let's think about our own life while we look to the lives of others. See what we can learn about becoming a man of influence.

The Qualities of a Man of Influence

Let's begin our list of qualities by looking at the life of the apostle Paul. Let's spend some time profiling the characteristics of this man's amazing life. Why Paul? Because Paul lived...

- a life of obedience to the Lord's commands

- a life of service to others

- a life of meekness and humility

- a life of prayer

- a life full of faith and trust

- a life of empowerment by the Spirit

- a life of loving and studying the Scriptures

- a life of modeling Christlikeness for others to follow

- a life of faithfulness to the end

Wouldn't you like to have this kind of a profile? I know I would! And God has given us Paul as a prime example to follow. What Christian man wouldn't want to live as powerfully as Paul did? By modeling our lives after this amazing man, you and I can have a great impact on our home, family, workplace, church, and neighborhood! As we look at how God worked through Paul (and others), let's determine together, from the start, to let God work in us and make some key changes in our lives.

This is my prayer for you and me:

that we would exhibit an open heart as we move through our profiling journey,

that we would be sensitive to the Lord's prompting as we examine the powerful life of Paul and others,

that we would be willing to make drastic changes if the Lord so directs, and

that we prayerfully ask God for a greater passion for living the Christian life.

Are you up for the challenge, my friend? I'm trusting that you are!

The Profile of a Man of Influence

Paul. Just say the name and a myriad of faces come to mind. For me, the name *Paul* reminds me of my two sons-in-law, both named Paul. For you, Paul may have been the name of an old buddy from days gone by. But as we begin our profiling journey, the Paul we are thinking about is the apostle Paul. Why Paul? What was so unique about his life that would make him worthy of our attention as a man of influence?

On the surface, Paul the apostle wasn't much of a physical specimen. One writer pictured him as "half-bald" and "bandy-legged."[3] A second-century church leader described Paul as "a man small of stature, with a bald head and crooked legs...with eyebrows meeting and nose somewhat hooked."[4] Well, friend, neither of these descriptions portrays Paul as a man of which legends are made.

No, it wasn't a commanding physical presence that made Paul such an outstanding Christian personality. It was his powerful life. And that's what we want to profile. Paul's life was characterized by love, compassion, peace, humility, focus, and numerous other noble qualities that made him a powerful force for the Christian faith, that made him a man of influence.

It's been said the apostle Paul was the most outstanding personality the Christian faith has ever produced.[5] That is an incredible statement to make about just one man out of the millions who have named the name of Christ as their Savior. Recently I re-read a book about Paul entitled *The Man Who Shook the World.*[6] This amazing title is used to describe the life of just one man among the myriads of believers who have lived down through the centuries of Chistendom. Clearly, Paul had a significant impact on the world around him.

As you and I profile the influential life of the apostle Paul through the lens of Scripture, we can't help but notice these accomplishments and more:

- *Paul wrote 13 God-inspired books of the New Testament.* The apostle John wrote five books, and the great apostle

Peter wrote only two. (Paul's feat seems more amazing when we consider that in his day, writing was done on animal skins and pressed reeds with quilled feathers, using a mixture of charcoal and water for ink.)

- *Paul's writings contributed many of the essential doctrinal truths of the Christian faith.* God communicated many foundational truths of Christianity through Paul, and the church has been able to build and grow on those truths over the last 1900 years (truths about justification by faith, the church as the Body of Christ, spiritual gifts, the deity of Christ, the resurrection, the return of Christ, and the kingdom of God, just to name a few).

- *Paul was a pioneer missionary and church planter.* Missionaries and church planters have spent the last 19 centuries patterning their strategies after Paul's effective and fruitful life and model. (As a former missionary, I have read numerous books that detail Paul's missionary journeys and their application for today.)

- *Paul was one of the great disciplers of men.* He raised up countless godly men to continue his work of ministry. Today we are still being challenged to fulfill the pattern set forth by Paul's admonition to one of his disciples—"The things you have heard me say in the presence of many witnesses entrust to reliable men who will also be qualified to teach others" (2 Timothy 2:2). (I have spent most of my adult Christian life following the pattern set by Paul in this verse—first, in my own training by "reliable men," and then by passing on that training to "others.")

The Path to a Life of Influence

However, there is a side of Paul and his life of influence that almost no one talks about: Paul's life was filled with *adversity*. He was constantly misunderstood by his fellow believers. He was relentlessly harassed by the enemies of the gospel. He spent many days, weeks, months, and even years in jails because of his faith. There are also a handful of additional facts about Paul's life and service to Christ that could be seen as "strikes" against him. If you or I ever think God cannot use us in mighty ways because of the adversities we have encountered, think again! If you ever get discouraged because of what seem to be "strikes" against you, think again! Remember the following facts about the path of Paul's life:

- *Paul did not become a Christian until he was more than 30 years old.* (The majority of people who become Christians come to Christ before the age of 15.)

- *Paul did not start his formal ministry until he was over 40.* (Most pastoral search committees would never consider the résumé of a man over 40 with little or no ministry experience! They are looking for a 40-year-old pastor with 15 to 20 years of pastoral experience. This standard would have caused the great and powerful apostle Paul to be passed over as a candidate for ministry.)

- *Paul did not make his first missionary journey until he was over 45.* (Many churches today send missionaries to the field right after they graduate from Bible school in their early twenties. Seldom do we send a middle-aged man to the mission field. We erroneously wonder, *What could he do? He's too old!* and fail to ask, "Who do you think is probably more mature, a man in his early twenties or a man in his early forties?")

- *Paul did not write his first book of the Bible until he was 49 years old.* (This was 15 years after his conversion. Those 15 years gave Paul time to mature in his faith and time to have something to say.) And, speaking of adversity, many of Paul's letters were written while he was a prisoner, chained to a Roman soldier!

- *Paul did not shun hardship and persecution.* His missionary travels of thousands of miles were mostly on foot or in crude, first-century sailing vessels. He also admits to frequent floggings, exposure to death, multiple imprisonments, five times receiving 39 lashes, beatings, and stonings...not to mention shipwrecks and the lack of a permanent home (2 Corinthians 11:23-27). (By the time most Christians reach their forties, they can't walk two miles, are already looking forward to retirement, and would define *hardship* as waiting 30 minutes to be seated at their favorite restaurant.)

In spite of getting a late start in the Christian life and the physical hardships he endured, Paul had a great impact! Paul's influence *began* when most men are beginning to pull out of the fast lane. What a challenge this should be to those of us who are getting on in age...say, 40! One loud lesson from Paul shouts across the centuries to you and me—*it's never too late to serve God.* No matter how difficult our circumstances, God can still use us.

The Pattern of Your Life

I trust this brief profile of "Paul of Tarsus" encourages you. (I know it encourages me!) Whatever your age or your situation, or the adversities you are experiencing or the number of "strikes" against you, with God's help, the best of your life and your greatest impact is yet to come. God shows us in the life of Paul that adversity is the seedbed He often uses to grow a man of influence.

Are you beginning to see why Paul's life and ministry are so unique and compelling? Already we are being challenged by this man's life, and we've just started! I'm sure you are as curious as I am as to what made this man tick. Well, take courage. We'll get there. We'll find the answers, and we'll find out what made other great men of influence tick as well.

But first…a word about you. If people were to profile and chronicle the pattern of your life, what would they see? Are there any contradictions? Are there any inconsistencies, any "blips on the screen"? Are there some "strikes" against you on your record? Is there a long list of suffering and adversity? Or does your date of birth reveal that time is running out, that not too many years are left, that perhaps you're a late bloomer?

If you're like me, the pattern of your life probably looks a little rocky. But be encouraged! You (and I) are in good company—the company of the apostle Paul. With God, all things are possible (Matthew 19:26). *He* is able to transform you into a man of influence, into a man whose life has a lasting impact on others and on the world!

> *He is no fool who gives what he cannot keep*
> *to gain what he cannot lose.*[7]
> —JIM ELLIOT

Taking the First Step Toward Influence

If anyone is in Christ, he is a new creation;
the old has gone, the new has come!
—2 Corinthians 5:17

Life is full of surprises…and usually we're not prepared for them. You and I never know when we get out of bed each morning what events during the day might end up having a marked effect on us, do we? And when surprises do hit us, we usually end up asking, "What happened?"

When it comes to encountering the unexpected, you're not alone. The apostle Paul experienced surprises as well. And one of those surprises turned his life completely around. One minute Paul was going in one direction, and in the next minute, his life was moving totally the opposite direction.

This causes us to wonder, *What happened?*

Paul was a bright and up-and-coming Jewish religious leader. He had an incredible mind and had been tutored by Gamaliel, the great Jewish leader and thinker (Acts 22:3). Yes, the young man Paul was destined to have a great impact upon Judaism. But a radical change took place that he didn't expect. What was it?

A Dramatic Encounter

Before we see what that surprise was, let's look at what led up to it. What was Paul (called Saul in the verses below) up to?

In the Bible, our first real introduction to Paul is in Acts chapter 9. There we read that "Saul was...breathing out murderous threats against the Lord's disciples." He had even gone to the high priest in Jerusalem and asked for letters to the synagogues in Damascus. Why the letters? So that Paul might take any and all Christians—both male and female—back to Jerusalem as prisoners (Acts 9:1-2).

Here's the scene: Paul was on his way from Jerusalem to Damascus, the ancient capital of Syria, some 100-plus miles to the north. The trek normally took about five or six days. Paul and his "henchmen" were almost to Damascus. They were within a day's journey. Paul was eager to get to the city and begin dealing with a group he considered to be heretics and a threat to the Jewish faith.

But God had other plans for Paul, the "hit man" for the high priest. "As he neared Damascus on his journey, suddenly a light from heaven flashed around him. He fell to the ground and heard a voice say to him, 'Saul, Saul, why do you persecute me?'"

"Who are you, Lord?" Saul asked.

"'I am Jesus, who you are persecuting,' he replied. 'Now get up and go into the city, and you will be told what you must do'" (Acts 9:3-6).

Needless to say, this dramatic encounter affected Paul's life. Truly, he was never the same! Paul saw, heard, and understood the voice of the Lord. The rest of his companions also saw the bright light and heard something, but they did not understand the voice (Acts 22:9). How can we explain this? We can't. And neither could Paul, who in the years to follow tried to comprehend and write about God's sovereign work in his life. All he could conclude was, "Oh, the depths of the riches of the wisdom and knowledge of God! How unsearchable his judgments, and his paths beyond tracing out!" (Romans 11:33).

A Sensational Reversal

Somewhere on the road to Damascus, somehow and at some moment (which no one can pinpoint), Paul became saved. He himself became one of those he was persecuting—a Christian. Paul's conversion was definitely dramatic, but the exact moment of salvation cannot be distinguished. Perhaps it was...

...when he heard the voice of the Lord,

...as he lay on the ground,

...when he was blinded,

...while he conversed with Christ, or

...during his three days of prayer and fasting while he awaited God's direction.

Whenever it was, Paul's life was changed so drastically that everyone took note. As you can see in the verses below, people had a hard time understanding Paul's transformation from a persecutor of Christians to a preacher of Christ:

> At once he began to preach in the synagogues that Jesus is the Son of God. All those who heard him were astonished and asked, "Isn't he the man who raised havoc in Jerusalem among those who call on this name? And hasn't he come here to take them as prisoners to the chief priests?" (Acts 9:20-21).

Dear reader, we, along with the people of Damascus, have just witnessed a sensational reversal in Paul's life. Knowing of his past, we are struck by the dramatic change that came over him. Paul went from killing Christians to leading people to Christ. What a complete transformation!

Yes, my friend, prior to this moment, Paul was having an impact. But it was a negative one, not a positive one. His influence went in the wrong direction.

The Direction of Your Influence

Before we move on, let's pause and ask, What is the direction of your influence? As we move through *God's Man of* ™ *Influence—Living a Life of Lasting Impact*, I will continually be reminding you to check the direction of your influence. Your influence is never neutral. You are having either a positive or a negative impact on others. In any and all of your relationships, as the following poem states, you are either leading others aright or astray. The choice is yours.

The Things I Do

The things I do,
The things I say,
Will lead some person
Aright or astray.
So the things we do
Should be the best,
And the things we say
Should be to bless.[8]

The Dramatic Nature of Your Conversion

The events surrounding Paul's conversion were most definitely out of the ordinary. God used a miraculous event to change the direction of Paul's life. It was so radical that Dr. Charles Swindoll entitled one of his chapters on Paul's life "The Violent Capture of a Rebel's Will."[9]

I don't know about you, but my conversion at the tender age of six didn't have any of the drama associated with Paul's experience. On the surface, you wouldn't describe my conversion as "the violent capture of a rebel's will." It *appears* that I was simply a young boy who needed a Savior and a boy who was fortunate to have a faithful mother who introduced me to that Savior at our family kitchen table while I was at home during my school lunch break.

From time to time, you and I may hear captivating testimonies from people who have been gloriously and dramatically saved from hideous or contrary lifestyles. But, like me, you probably had a conversion that *appears* (there's that word again!) to be a less-than-sensational event.

Well, an "ordinary" conversion may seem to be an uneventful occurrence on the *human* plane. But, my friend, in the *spiritual* realm, your conversion and mine are anything but ordinary or uneventful! I, like Paul, was a rebel (even at six years old!). And so were you! Our conversion, or re-creation (2 Corinthians 5:17), is an incredible and dramatic event, rivaling even that of Creation itself. And our conversion is just as dynamic as anyone's when we consider these terrifying truths:

- We were spiritually dead in our transgressions and sins (Ephesians 2:1).

- We were children of disobedience—rebels (Ephesians 2:2).

- We were children of wrath (Ephesians 2:3).

- We were separated from Christ (Ephesians 2:12).

- We were without hope and without God in the world (Ephesians 2:12).

We were in a pretty hopeless state. I repeat, we were rebels! We were separated from God on this earth. And to die in this state would mean eternal separation from God. And what's more, *we didn't even care!*

A Divine Intervention

"But...God" (Ephesians 2:4).

What an incredible statement! *God* initiated a rescue. Paul was on his way to Damascus (and to hell!), doing what he thought was God's will...

"But...God."

Before salvation, we too were on our way through life, hoping, like Paul did, that somehow, in some way, our "good" or "righteous" or "religious" deeds would earn us entrance into God's heaven. But salvation doesn't work that way. *Man's* formula requires man to take the initiative to effect his own salvation. *God's* formula, however, is "But...God." Read it for yourself.

> *But* because of his great love for us, *God*, who
> is rich in *mercy*, made us alive with Christ even
> when we were dead in transgressions—it is by
> *grace* you have been saved (Ephesians 2:4-5).

God's mercy and God's grace intervened in the life of Paul. And, my friend, God's mercy and God's grace intervened in your life, too, if you have trusted Christ as your Lord and Savior.

Let's pause again for a moment. What does this mean, that God's mercy and God's grace intervened in our behalf? Remember, you and I were enemies of God (Romans 5:10), just like Paul.

But...God...

- rescued us from the dominion of darkness (Colossians 1:13),

- brought us into the kingdom of the Son (Colossians 1:13),

- saved us through faith (Ephesians 2:8),

- forgave us our sins (Colossians 1:14),

- made us spiritually alive together with Christ (Ephesians 2:5),

- seated us with Him in the heavenly realms in Christ Jesus (Ephesians 2:6), and

- sealed us with the Spirit (2 Corinthians 1:22).

All we can say, along with the hymnwriter, is "Hallelujah, what a Savior!"[10]

Now, friend, the next time you hear of someone's "dramatic conversion" or read of a startling salvation experience like Paul's, remember this—you, too, had a dramatic conversion. Remember that Christ's payment for sin was just as great for you as it was for Paul, the rebel, or for any other person who puts their faith in the risen Lord Jesus Christ. *Every* conversion is dramatic! Whether you were a rebel like Paul, or a tender child like Paul's associate Timothy (2 Timothy 1:5), or a hardened warden like the Philippian jailer (Acts 16:29), *every* conversion is dramatic!

The First Step to a Life of Influence

You know, it just occurred to me that maybe I'm running a bit ahead of you here. Maybe you haven't yet experienced God's grace and mercy in your life. Maybe you haven't received Him as your Lord and Savior. If not, you can take the first step to a life of influence right now—the same first step Paul had to take—by uttering a heartfelt prayer like this one:

> Jesus, I know I am a sinner, but I want to repent of my sins and turn to follow You. I believe You died for my sins and rose again victorious over the power of sin and death, and I want to accept You as my personal Savior. Come into my life, Lord Jesus, and help me obey You from this day forward.

Truly, opening your heart to Jesus Christ is the first step to a life of influence! Whether you took that step this moment or at some time in the past, having Jesus Christ as the driving force in your life will ensure that you will have a positive impact on those who come in contact with you.

Now...back to where we left off with Paul. The great Paul, the persecutor of Christians, was now a believer. Paul was "a new creation." His past was gone—it was history! He had been given a second chance...and his new life in Christ was ahead of him. Truly, as the Bible explains it, the old was gone and the new had begun (2 Corinthians 5:17).

We must stop and mark this well—Paul's usefulness to God began with his salvation. Every truly godly element of Paul's life, every truly righteous quality, began that day on the Damascus Road. And, my profiling friend, that's where it begins with you and me as well.

You and I cannot have a godly, righteous influence by our own human efforts. And we cannot have a godly, righteous influence without first meeting the Savior and coming under His influence. I know I am repeating myself, but it's vitally important: Have *you*, my new friend, met the risen Savior Jesus Christ? Has He given *you* a new beginning? If you want a life of influence—a life lived for the glory of God—then you must begin that life with Jesus.

Paul's life of influence was launched when he met the Master face to face on that dusty road to Damascus. And from then on, Paul's life was never the same. Nor is any man who meets Jesus ever the same. You too must meet the Master face to face. That's the first step to a life of influence. As you read the poetic testimony on the next page, ask yourself if you've met the Master.

I had walked life's way with an easy tread,
I had traveled where pleasures and comfort led.
Until one day in a quiet place,
I met the Master face to face.

With station and rank and wealth for my goal,
Much thought for my body but none for my soul,
I had entered to win this life's mad race,
When I met the Master face to face.

I built my castles and reared them high,
Till their towers had pierced the blue of the sky;
I had sworn to rule with an iron mace,
When I met the Master face to face.

I met Him, and knew Him and blushed to see,
That His eyes full of sorrow were fixed upon me;
I faltered and fell at His feet that day,
While my castles melted and vanished away.
Melted and vanished and in their place,
Nothing else could I see but the Master's face.

My thoughts are now for the souls of men,
I've lost my life to find it again;
Ever since that day in a quiet place,
Where I met the Master face to face.[11]

> *Obedience to God's will is the secret of*
> *spiritual knowledge and insight.*
> *It is not willingness to know,*
> *but willingness to do God's will*
> *that brings certainty.*
> —ERIC LIDDELL[12]

3

LIVING A LIFE OF OBEDIENCE

I was not disobedient to the vision from heaven.
—ACTS 26:19

Imagine that it's sometime in the future. Life is different. *Very* different! You are no longer living in a Christian-friendly society. Believers in Christ are routinely persecuted and humiliated. Christianity is under attack by the forces of evil. The Christian faith is in a fight for its life. And there you are, in your home, minding your own business, just trying to keep a low profile. You're in a comfortable chair reading a book—or your Bible—and you are contemplating how God has protected you and your family up to this point.

Suddenly a knock comes at the front door...or the phone rings. It's someone you respect very much—your pastor. And he's asking you to do the unthinkable...the impossible...to seek out the man who's responsible for much of the persecution that's taking place. You (yes, you!) are to bring that man a message from God. And, I mean, this man *hates* Christians!

Christian man, whether you realize it or not, you've just come face to face with a test of your obedience to God. How will you respond?

We'll return to this scenario later. For now, though, hold on to that question while we turn our attention back to what it takes to become a man of influence.

To Obey or Not to Obey...

...that is the question. And every man must answer it, including you and me and the men whose stories follow. Before we do so, however, I'd like to share with you how some men in the Bible responded.

Paul—We've already witnessed Paul's experience on the Damascus Road. But there's more! Struck blind and lying in the dirt, Paul's first words to his new Master were, "What shall I do, Lord?" (Acts 22:10). And Paul's first orders from the Master were, "Get up and go into the city, and you will be told what you must do" (Acts 9:6). Paul had a choice—to obey or not to obey. That was the question.

As we catalog the qualities that made Paul's life such a powerful instrument in the hands of God, we must quickly add obedience to that list. Obedience was a part of Paul's profile. And Paul's life was a life of power and influence because Paul's life was a life of obedience.

How long was Paul obedient to His Savior? Was it a day? A week? A month? Even a year? Answer: A man of influence is a man of God whose obedience is without question, without hesitation, and at any cost...for life. Thirty years after Paul became a Christian, he boldly declared when on trial for his faith, "I was not disobedient to the vision from heaven" (Acts 26:19). In other words, from the day—even the second!—Paul experienced his miraculous supernatural encounter with Christ, he had complied with whatever God asked of him.

Now you may be thinking to yourself, *Paul's standard is too high for me. I can never be this kind of man. In fact, my life is far from where it needs to be.* Well, friend, you're not alone. I look at Paul's life and I too see how far I need to go. But you and I have to start somewhere. So let's start by asking ourselves this simple but penetrating question:

Are there any areas of disobedience in your life that you need to deal with? If there are, I beg you to give them up! Hand them over to God! Be done with them. Get on with realizing the potential of your life as a Christian man, with living a life of influencing others.

Maybe you've had a time off, or a time out, or a time away from the Lord. Maybe your track record with God isn't as great or as smooth or as consistent as you would have liked. But don't give up. It's never too late. God's hands are always stretched out to His people (Romans 10:21), ready to help them.

Others—Obedience is not unique to Paul's life. The Bible contains numerous other examples of men of influence—men who were asked to obey God, even in what seemed impossible circumstances. For instance,

- Abraham was asked to sacrifice his only son (Genesis 22:2)...and Abraham obeyed God.

- Moses was asked to confront Pharaoh and lead God's people out of Egypt (Exodus 3:10)...and Moses obeyed God.

- Daniel was asked to stop worshiping God or be thrown into the lion's den (Daniel 6:8-10)...and Daniel obeyed God instead.

All these men had two things in common. First, they were obedient in the midst of seemingly impossible situations. And second, their obedience equipped them to live powerful and influential lives. Just look at their influence!

- Abraham's son was spared, and Abraham was greatly blessed by God. He was known as a great leader in his day, and his descendants became the great nation of Israel. God told Abraham, "Through your offspring [Jesus] all nations on earth will be blessed," and the Bible goes on to say why: "because you have obeyed me" (Genesis 22:18).

- Moses' obedience qualified him to lead the nation of Israel out of Egypt and to the promised land. God gave this tribute to Moses: "My servant Moses…is faithful in all my house" (Numbers 12:7).

• Daniel was thrown into the lion's den, but God miraculously closed the mouths of the lions. Daniel's king publicly glorified God as a result of the miracle, and Daniel continued to enjoy great success as a leader (Daniel 6:28), receiving numerous visions about the future because of his life of obedience.

Dear friend, each of these men was asked by God to do something. In short, Paul was asked to *get up*, Abraham was asked to *give up*, Moses was asked to *speak up*, and Daniel was asked to *stand up*. Is God asking for your obedience in any of these ways? Is He asking you to *get up* out of your La-Z-Boy chair and be more involved with your family or church? Is there something God may be asking you to *give up*—something you love that is standing between you and complete obedience and service to God? Or is there some person—or some issue—God would have you *speak up* to as a witness about the things of God? Or is there some practice in your family or at work that you should *stand up* to, or take a stand against? You and I join the ranks of the great men in the Bible when we follow God in obedience.

Ananias—There's one more example of obedience we simply cannot pass over. He was a guy just like you and me. If you're having trouble identifying with Paul, Abraham, Moses, and Daniel, this is the man for you! His is the story of an ordinary, insignificant (by most standards) man who was asked to do the impossible (or so it seemed!). Most men probably have not heard of him. His name was Ananias.

Ananias is a classic example of a man who displayed obedience in the midst of a difficult situation. The details of his obedience are found right in the middle of the story of Paul's conversion. In fact, Ananias's obedience was a part of that story.

Ananias was a Jewish believer who lived in Damascus. Whatever *his* reasons for being in Damascus were, God had *His* own reasons. For it was there that Ananias received the greatest test of his life...and his faith—a test not unlike the imaginary test you were given at the beginning of this chapter.

Do you remember the fictional opening story for this chapter—about bringing a message from God to a person who hates Christianity? I asked, "How would you respond?" We now know how Paul, Abraham, Moses, and Daniel responded to hard situations. They obeyed! But Ananias? Let's learn now how this reluctant disciple responded.

> In Damascus there was a disciple named Ananias. The Lord called to him in a vision, "Ananias!"
>
> "Yes, Lord," he answered.
>
> The Lord told him, "Go to the house of Judas on Straight Street and ask for a man from Tarsus named Saul, for he is praying. In a vision he has seen a man named Ananias come and place his hands on him to restore his sight" (Acts 9:10-12).

Ananias did what you and I would probably have done in our imaginary situation at the beginning of this chapter—he tried to reason his way out of obedience.

But Lord, you don't understand.

Now listen in on the dialogue between the Lord and Ananias. Try to put yourself in Ananias's sandals.

> "Lord," Ananias answered, "I have heard many reports about this man and all the harm he has done to your saints in Jerusalem. And he has come here with authority from the chief priests to arrest all who call on your name" (Acts 9:13-14).

Now, you and I know that the Lord didn't need a lecture. And He didn't need to be reminded of what kind of man Paul was. His command to Ananias was, "Go." There was no way Ananias could misinterpret the command. It was unmistakable. And Ananias had to decide—to obey, or not to obey? (There's that question again!) Would he trust the Lord? Would he obey God and go in spite of what he knew about Paul? Or would he choose to disobey the Lord?

Luke, the writer of the book of Acts, wastes no words in describing what happened next. He reports, "So Ananias departed" (Acts 9:17 NASB). And, as the saying goes, the rest is history! Humanly speaking, the obedience of this one man, Ananias, started a chain reaction of events that has marked the world and the expansion of the church to this very day. But this seemingly insignificant man's singular influence all started with his willingness to obey. His obedience made him a significant and influential force in church history.

Ananias became a man of great influence because he was obedient in the small things. His impact grew one step at a time. Here's Ananias's example to us:

- *Be available*—When the Lord called, Ananias said, "Yes, Lord."

- *Be willing*—When the Lord had finished giving Ananias His instructions, in spite of Ananias's reluctance, he departed.

- *Be prepared*—When the challenge was given, Ananias went ahead, ready to accept the consequences of his obedience. He knew Paul could mean harm to him, but he obeyed God's call to go see Paul.

- *Be expectant*—When Ananias willingly left to meet Paul, not only was Ananias prepared for the consequences, but he also went with full confidence, expecting God to work through his obedience. "Jesus...has sent me so that you may see again" (Acts 9:17).

You—I know we've talked a lot in this chapter about you and your obedience. And you may be thinking, *I can't measure up to men like Abraham and Paul.* But we must realize that these "heroes" of the faith were just common, ordinary men like you and me. Their obedience, however, gave them an uncommon strength for the glory of God. I don't know about you, but examples like these motivate me to re-evaluate my own obedience. Am I being asked by God to do what seems to be impossible? And because it seems to be impossible, am I wavering in the all-important area of obedience, failing to be available and willing...prepared and expectant?

The Power of Obedience

There will never be another apostle Paul. (His exploits are many!) And leaders like Abraham, Moses, and Daniel are few and far between. But you and I can definitely be another Ananias. All it takes is a desire to faithfully obey the commands of Scripture as they are presented. We may be reluctant at times—Ananias was. But if we are ultimately faithful to follow God's commands, we too can have a powerful and lasting impact on those around us.

So as followers of Christ, the question to you and me is simple—*to obey...or not obey?* As we profile the lives of great men of God throughout this book, we will observe over and over again that obedience was the ingrained pattern of their life, an obvious habit that marked them, a secret that made them men of influence and lasting impact.

Where does a life of obedience lead us? Read on in the next chapter and see how obedience can lead us down a path of joy and discovery.

Do you know what I believe is the icing on the cake of obedience, what I believe to be one of the most compelling reasons for our obedience? It is this: obedience leads to a powerful, confident life. When you and I are obedient, and when we allow ourselves to be led by God through the unexpected, we then have a confidence based on the fact that we know we are exactly where God wants us to be. What a joy it is to know we are in the center of God's will!

—JIM GEORGE

4

FOLLOWING THE PATH OF OBEDIENCE

After Paul had seen the vision,
we got ready at once to leave for Macedonia,
concluding that God had called us
to preach the gospel to them.

—ACTS 16:10

My little grandson Jacob is a great fan of the children's cartoon character Bob the Builder. Jacob has a plastic Bob the Builder hard hat, a Bob the Builder T-shirt, and a computer game in which he and Bob the Builder build something together. For us guys, the bent toward building gets into our blood early, doesn't it? We build all kinds of things. We build houses and furniture. We also build careers, companies, and financial assets. We are constantly building something or other.

But, as we've been learning, there is something far more important for us to be concerned about building. I'm referring to building a life of influence. I trust that as you've been reading along, you have been paying close attention to the secrets of building a life of influence and lasting impact.

So far we have seen that true influence starts by laying a firm foundation with Jesus Christ. No man's life can have a true and lasting impact without taking this essential first step. Then in our last chapter we saw that influence for God comes as we erect a proper spiritual life through obedience to God. By now your life's structure should be taking shape. The frame for your building should be going up. But the construction process has just begun! Now, let's switch metaphors and continue our travels and look at where the path of obedience leads us.

The Path of Obedience

I'm sure by now you know what a powerful influence the life of Paul has had on me and on many others (and hopefully you, too!). I can't help but ask you to take another look at Paul's walk of obedience as we continue to determine what's involved in becoming a man of influence. And I want us to pick up our journey with Paul and travel alongside him again for a time. As we fast-forward in his life, we are no longer accompanying Paul on the well-traveled Damascus Road of Syria. In fact, 20 years have passed. This time, we're going to walk beside him on a dusty back road located in what is now north-central Turkey. Paul is there because he is continuing to obey his Lord's commands to take the gospel message to the Gentiles.

Paul is now in his mid-fifties. And he's well into the second of three long and hard missionary trips. This journey will last more than three years. And Paul's obedience has not been without a price. He has been scourged countless times. He has been stoned and left for dead. He has been imprisoned in many of the towns where he has preached. Yet Paul continues to follow the path of obedience. Where does the less-traveled path of obedience lead?

To discover the exciting answers to that question I want you to do two things. First, read the Bible passage below. Then follow along with Paul through these verses to see where the path of obedience led him...and can lead you and me as well.

> Paul and his companions traveled throughout the region of Phrygia and Galatia, having been kept by the Holy Spirit from preaching the word in the province of Asia. When they came to the border of Mysia, they tried to enter Bithynia, but the Sprit of Jesus would not allow

them to. So they passed by Mysia and went down to Troas. During the night Paul had a vision of a man of Macedonia standing and begging him, "Come over to Macedonia and help us." After Paul had seen the vision, we got ready at once to leave for Macedonia, concluding that God had called us to preach the gospel to them (Acts 16:6-10).

Obedience often leads to the unexpected—We don't know how God communicated to Paul and his missionary team. But we do know that "they were kept by the Holy Spirit from preaching the word in the province of Asia" and that "the Spirit of Jesus would not allow them" to continue to move in the direction they were traveling (verses 6-7).

As a result of God's prohibitions, Paul and his faithful companions in ministry were diverted from their intended destination in the northern region of Galatia and led instead to Troas, a city to the west. They were expecting to go north...but ended up going west.

Something similar happened to my friend Marty. (Marty, by the way, is the father-in-law of my editor and friend, Steve Miller.) Marty believed God was calling him and his family to minister in France. Therefore he started language training and prepared to go to France. But God had other plans. Marty was expecting to minister in France, but he ended up using his French to minister to the people of Montreal, Canada. As Marty was obedient to God, he experienced the unexpected.

How about you? Are you fearful because God is moving you in an unexpected direction? Is the unknown causing you to waver on the path of obedience? Take heart in your resolve. Walk in confidence with God. Walk as King David did, declaring, "Even though I walk through the valley of the shadow of death, I will fear no evil, for you are with me" (Psalm 23:4).

Like Paul and his team, you and I don't always know where God's will may take us. Oh, we may think we do! But often our obedience will lead us to the unexpected. And that's okay, for that's exactly where God wants us. *Often the center of God's will lies in the unexpected.*

Obedience often leads to clarification—As Paul and his men chose to continue to obey God's leading, God's will and direction for their lives became clearer and clearer. It was as if God was saying, "Hey, no, guys! It's not *that* direction...it's *this* direction!" The missionaries thought they were to evangelize the northern cities of Asia Minor. But with obedience came clear direction to leave Asia and to instead witness to the people of Macedonia (known today as Greece), a totally different region off to the west.

If Paul and his men had stopped at any point along the way, they might not have fully realized God's complete plan for their lives and ministry. Think again of my friend Marty. As Marty continued to follow the Lord's direction, his ministry destination was further clarified. What an influence Marty and his family had upon the people of Montreal! Why? Because Marty continued to heed God's direction, allowing God to work and to reveal His will at the right time.

I've had this happen in my own life as well. After our family returned from a time of missionary service in Singapore, I was at a crossroads. I thought I was to seek a pulpit ministry. So I applied for numerous pastoral positions. However, I was always the second-favorite candidate. I was getting pretty frustrated. I thought this was what God was calling me to, so why was this happening over and over again? Then one day, in the midst of my frustration (or should I say my lack of trust?), I was asked to join the faculty at Talbot School of Theology in Southern California.

Looking back, I can see how God was directing me through "closed" and "open" doors. He had a purpose for me at Talbot, and that led to other things. Even now I can see God continuing to clarify the direction of my life as I am obedient to follow His will. And much to my surprise, His power is always most evident when I willingly and obediently allow Him to make clear the path before me.

Are you beginning to see why obedience is such an important part of living a life of influence? You and I will never fully know the will of God and the power of God in our lives without obedience. *Obedience clarifies God's will.*

Obedience leads us as we listen—During the formative years of Christianity, before the New Testament was in written form, Jesus often communicated with the fledgling church through visions and dreams. We've already witnessed this in God's guidance of Paul and Ananias, as mentioned in earlier chapters, and now here it is again. The Bible doesn't say how God communicated with Paul and his team, whether by visions, dreams, or a voice, or even by a prophet like Agabus (Acts 11:27-28). But we do know Paul and his crew were sensitive to the Spirit's leading and they listened to God obediently. They desired God's will and looked for it. And when it came, they listened. As a result, they were led by God until they ended up with God's final directive—a vision of a man from the region of Macedonia begging them to come there.

The Provisions for Obedience

Now, the question for you and me is, How do *we* receive our directions from God today? God speaks to us through what I call "the four C's":

C-ommands from the inspired Word of God

C-ompetent and wise counselors

C-ircumstances and changing conditions

C-onscience aided by the Holy Spirit

Friend, at one time or another, God uses any or all of these means to give direction to you and me. In my case, God used the wise counsel of my pastor and guidance from some close friends as I struggled with whether to continue pursuing a pulpit ministry or to accept a seminary teaching position.

Whether you are a pastor, a plumber, a painter, young or old, a Paul or a new Christian, you need to ask yourself: Am I listening as God speaks to me through some or all of these means? You will never know the will of God if you are not sensitive to God's Spirit and therefore tune out His voice, which may come through any of these different avenues. How can I say this with such certainty? Because...

- You can never obey a command that you never read in the Bible.

- You can never obey godly advice that you never ask for or accept.

- You can never obey God's leading through circumstances and changes if you are not willing to obey in the midst of those circumstances and changes.

- You can never obey the Spirit's leading if you are not listening with a heart that's willing to obey.

Obedience to the will of God is possible only as we listen when God speaks to us through any of these four means of communication. *Are you listening?*

Obedience leads us one decision at a time—Question: How did Paul get to the point in his life where he was looking across the Aegean Sea toward a new mission field? Answer: He arrived at it...one act of obedience at a time. Paul's path of obedience started on the Damascus Road. But it didn't stop there. As soon as Paul could see...he was obedient to be baptized. And it didn't stop there. As soon as he regained his strength...

he began to preach. And it didn't stop there. It continued on, one step at a time...until Paul could reflect back on more than 25 years as a Christian and state before kings, "I was not disobedient to the vision" (Acts 26:19).

Dear brother, your influence on the lives of others—your family, the people at your church, your workmates—is cultivated with each life-decision you make. It's the little things—such as reading your Bible, praying, going to church, and standing up for your faith at work—that add influence to your life. Obey God one decision at a time and see where it leads you. Always remember: *The key to a powerful Christian life is obedience to our Lord's leading—one decision at a time.*

Obedience leads to confident living—As we've already seen, Paul and Company finally made it to Troas, where they received the vision of the man from Macedonia. Then these words— "we got ready *at once* to leave for Macedonia"—were used to describe the group's eagerness to obey God's leading once they understood the command (Acts 16:10). (Don't fail to notice their teachable spirit...as well as their *confident* spirit!)

Now comes the icing on the cake—what I believe to be one of the most compelling reasons for our obedience. It is this: Obedience leads to a powerful, confident life. When you and I are obedient, and when we allow ourselves to be led by God through the unexpected, we then have a confidence based on the fact that we know we are exactly where God wants us to be. What a joy it is to know we are in the center of God's will! Then we, along with Paul, can confidently lead and boldly influence others as we declare, "Follow my example, as I follow the example of Christ" (1 Corinthians 11:1). Indeed, *obedience leads to a powerful, confident life.*

A Desire to Be Obedient

Now, how about you? Wouldn't you like to have that kind of confidence in your life? Wouldn't you like to live a powerful and influential life? Wouldn't you like your life to have a lasting impact and give glory to God?

If your answer is yes (and I can't imagine why it wouldn't be!), then ask God to give you the strength to obey His commands as they come to you. And how will God's commands come? They will come...

...as you faithfully read His Word,

...as you faithfully hear the preaching of His Word,

...as you faithfully listen to wise counsel from His Word, and

...as you faithfully deal with sin in your life as revealed by the piercing light of His Word.

A desire to obediently follow the Lord's leading *should* be the supreme goal of your life. Is it? Your willingness to trust and obey the Lord is a key step toward experiencing God's blessings in your life. And it is a key element in becoming a man of influence.

With that in mind, let *your* heart sing the words of the beloved, time-honored hymn of commitment to obedience that appears on the next page.

Trust and Obey

When we walk with the Lord

in the light of His Word,

What a glory He sheds on our way!

While we do His good will

He abides with us still,

And with all who will trust and obey.

Trust and obey,

For there's no other way

To be happy in Jesus,

But to trust and obey.[13]

A university professor noticed a student was about to fall asleep in class. So the teacher asked the student, "What is the greatest problem in our society—ignorance or apathy?" The student replied, "I don't know and I don't care."[14]

Mastering Life's Challenges

*Judge for yourselves
whether it is right in God's sight
to obey you rather than God.*
—Acts 4:19

As a boy growing up in Oklahoma in the 1950s, I, like most of my friends, loved football. I even tried out for my local high school squad. Well, my lessons in humility began right then and there—I was cut before the end of the first week of tryouts!

Not wanting to give up on my athletic aspirations, I next tried running the hurdles on the track team. Timing was everything. To clear each hurdle, I had to run as hard as I could for an exact number of steps, then jump…and hope to clear the hurdle. I have to report (with even more humility) that the challenge of the hurdles was too much for me. I settled for running the half-mile and the mile (and still run to this day).

My brief attempt at jumping hurdles is a good illustration of what can happen as we seek to commit ourselves to a life of obedience. We *want* to obey God…but along comes a hurdle. At that point, we have a choice: We can decide it's not worth the effort and give up, or we can continue down the path of obedience and learn the secret of doing what it requires to master and take the hurdles one by one as they come. Let's consider how we can master the challenges, the hurdles, that are certain to arise in our attempt to live a life of obedience.

The Church Began with Challenges

To begin, realize you and I are in good company! From the very beginning of the church, the early disciples faced challenges. Their first challenge was to choose whether they would serve the risen Christ or bow to the pressures of the religious leaders of their day. Even before Paul's relentless persecution of the church, Peter and John, two of Jesus' twelve disciples, were called before the Sanhedrin, the main religious counsel in Israel. There, they were seriously threatened and commanded to stop preaching in the name of Jesus.

What happened? These men of God—and men whose influence for Christ has reached across the past 2000 years—resisted. How? They courageously declared, "Judge for yourselves whether it is right in God's sight to obey you rather than God. For we cannot help speaking about what we have seen and heard" (Acts 4:19-20).

The path of obedience is seldom easy. And it wasn't easy for the first disciples in the church. But the faithful band of early believers resisted the challenge to disobey their risen Savior's command to be His witnesses (Acts 1:8).

And what was the effect of their obedience? "They were all filled with the Holy Spirit and spoke the word of God boldly" (Acts 4:31). Their obedience was fueled by the power of the Holy Spirit, and their influence was felt even to the ends of the earth (Acts 1:8). Now *that's* influence! May you and I courageously master the challenges that come our way and follow the pattern of obedience set by these men of old!

This seems like a good place to pause and ask, Who are you serving, my friend? The risen Savior, or someone (or something) else? Are you making an effort to clear the hurdles before you? Are you standing firm in obedience? And are you standing up for your Christian beliefs? Jesus Christ was the beginning of the church, and He is the beginning (and the end!) of the life of every man of influence. To have a lasting impact for Christ and to leave an indelible mark on this world, you too must obey Christ and master the challenges.

The Challenges of Obedience

As we've already seen, obedience wasn't easy for Paul and his men. Paul's path was riddled with challenges. He and his team of missionaries had (and would!) face many challenges to their faith. No, obedience is never easy. In fact, it's downright hard! But obedience is what God asked of Paul and his men. And obedience was what God asked of the early disciples. And, my friend, if we are to be men of influence, obedience is what God is asking of us—even with all its challenges.

Obedience to God always has its challenges. Maybe this is why it's the less-traveled path. Disobedience, on the other hand, seems to be the more traveled, more well-worn path. In fact, it is characterized by gridlock! Why? Because disobedience is the easy path. It's the path we're tempted to take when things get sticky. It's the path with the least challenges. And sadly, it's the path that makes us men of little or no influence.

What are some of the challenges that we face in our quest to be men of influence? As we run the race for Christ, what are the hurdles that trip us up, knock us down, or pressure us to compromise and rationalize what we know to be God's standards? And how can you and I overcome and master these challenges and keep moving onward in our desire to become men of influence?

I'm sure you probably have a few "pet" challenges in your own life. As I share a few of mine—a few that have bothered and derailed my life over the years—you will probably find yourself thinking of some of your own challenges.

The challenge of ignorance—One of the most tragic challenges to obedience and godly influence is ignorance—about the commands of Scripture. We live in a day and age of biblical illiteracy. Christian men, I'm sad to say, are particularly ignorant about spiritual truths. Knowing God's Word just doesn't seem to be the "manly" thing to do. Many men don't know what the Bible has to say about the issues and struggles they face every day. Such ignorance causes us to fail to live boldly for Christ.

And such ignorance costs us, too—I know! I know it from an experience I had several years ago: Even though I was only driving 35 miles an hour, I was pulled over by a policeman for speeding. I tried to explain to the officer that I didn't see the sign that read "School Zone—20 Miles Per Hour." How far did my plea of ignorance get me with that officer? You guessed it—a $120 fine!

God, too, has a standard of conduct for His men. And brother, the Bible contains that standard. On at least four occasions Paul begged his readers to not be *ignorant* of God's plans.[15] Let's heed Paul's admonition...and his heart. He pleaded, "I do not want you to be *ignorant*" (Romans 11:25). In other words, Paul (like the police officer) is saying ignorance is no excuse.

Having taught at a seminary for so many years, I can't resist giving a quick pop quiz!

- On a scale of 1 to 10, how would you rate your knowledge of God's Word?

- On a scale of 1 to 10, how would you rate your knowledge of your local or favorite sports team?

- Which had the higher rating, your sports team or God's Word?

Maybe you're not into sports. Then I invite you to rate your knowledge of God's Word against whatever it is that can easily divert your attention. Then ask yourself the same question: Which had the higher score?

Are you getting the picture? Your Christian influence comes from the power of God's Word, not from your knowledge of the things of this world. If you want to be a man of influence, you cannot be ignorant of the Bible's teachings. As D.L. Moody, preacher-of-old and influencer-of-many, put it, "I never met a useful Christian who was not a student of the Bible."[16]

The challenge of the flesh—Every Christian man would agree that the presence of sin in our world is a fact of life that challenges our obedience. From the second that sin entered the world through Adam and Eve's disobedience, all mankind (including you and me) entered into a struggle with obedience. Sometimes that struggle is with God and His Word. Sometimes it's with governmental authority and laws—laws like speed limits, our bosses, or our own conscience.

Friend, *every* man battles with the flesh...even the great apostle Paul. As you read below from the book of Romans, sense the conflict between Paul's sinful flesh and his desire to obey God. (And take note that Paul was in his late fifties when he wrote these words. Mastering the flesh is a lifelong battle!) But don't miss the victory. There is hope for us!

> So I find this law at work: When I want to do good, evil is right there with me. For in my inner being I delight in God's law; but I see another law at work in the members of my body, waging war against the law of my mind and making me a prisoner of the law of sin at work within my members. What a wretched man I am! Who will rescue me from this body of death? Thanks be to God—through Jesus Christ our Lord! (Romans 7:21-24).

Yes, the battles of the flesh are real. But you can master your flesh—rather than letting it master you! Here are some practical steps to **M-A-S-T-E-R** the challenges of the flesh.

M-onitor your time with those who drag you down, whether they be friends, workmates, or family.

A-ccount for your struggles to a more spiritually mature man or possibly your wife.

S-trengthen your inner man by the study of God's Word
and through prayer.

T-rain your eyes to avoid anything that might fan the
flames of your fleshly desires.

E-xercise purity in all your relationships with women.

R-un from the lusts of the flesh.

The challenge of apathy—Ignorance breeds apathy. And
apathy for a Christian man—a man meant to live boldly for
Christ—is like dying of hypothermia, like freezing to death.
When you and I are exposed too long to the cold winds of
ignorance and compromise, we slowly drift through complacency into the icy death of apathy. The book of Revelation
describes this drift into apathy as being "lukewarm—neither
hot nor cold" (Revelation 3:16).

Apathy is not just a modern-day spiritual challenge. (Just
read the book of Judges, where the people of Israel struggled
repeatedly with complacency!) Given the distractions and
temptations all around us, it's easy for us to flirt with apathy.
We go our own way. We become cold and hardened to the ways
of God. We begin to live our life as "practical atheists." We start
living as if there is no God (or at least a God we are accountable to). Then, one day, surprise of surprises(!), we get into
trouble…and *then* we cry out to God to bail us out. Suddenly
we are eager to obey God's commands, but not until our apathy
has led us down the path of disobedience and its resultant pain
and consequences.

Apathy is such a subtle challenge. In fact, it is so subtle that
I didn't even see it coming until it was too late. Let me explain.
I went away to college to study to be a pharmacist. I fully
intended to continue my habit of going to church and being
active in student ministry. However, little by little I stopped
going to church on a regular basis. I was too busy with college
life and my studies to be involved with other Christians at

church activities. Eventually I got to the point where I was "spiritually frozen." For the next 10 years I was in the grips of spiritual apathy. I was useless to God. I was barren of any spiritual life and fruit. I was even having a *negative* influence on others because of my apathy.

It's sobering, isn't it? You and I better believe it—apathy is deadly! And none of us are immune to it. I wasn't, and you aren't immune to its icy touch either. I hope you never end up at the same point I reached. How did I survive apathy? It was the grace of God that came to my aid.

Friend, apathy is a heart condition. It turns your heart for God into a heart that thinks it can exist without God. How do you keep from drifting into spiritual apathy? How can you keep apathy from settling into your life? Check your spiritual temperature on a regular basis by asking these questions:

Am I making excuses for missing church?

Am I becoming comfortable with little sins?

Am I able to take or leave God's Word?

Am I spending more of my discretionary hours with non-Christians rather than Christians?

Am I looking to myself or the world rather than to God for help with life issues?

Am I resisting the warnings of fellow believers?

If your answer to any or most of these questions is *yes*, then, my brother, you are well on your way to apathy. But realize that with God's help, you can overcome the problem. Speaking as a pharmacist, here is my "spiritual prescription" for dealing with apathy.

℞   Recognize that apathy can happen to you.

℞   Realize that God's Word is essential.

Rx   Reach out to those with "hot hearts" for the Lord.

Rx   Regularly attend church.

Rx   Request that others hold you accountable for your commitments to God.

Mastering Life's Challenges

Ignorance, the flesh, and apathy—these are definitely three challenges that can cause Christian men to stumble on the path to becoming men of influence! But the three keys to mastering these three challenges are:

- acknowledging the challenges of ignorance, the flesh, and apathy,

- looking to God for help, and

- taking appropriate action.

Friend, do you see it? Ultimately it's *you* who determines if you want to be ignorant of God's Word. It's *you* who decides if you want to give in to the flesh. It's *you* who dictates whether you drift into apathy. All three of these challenges can be mastered as *you* look to God for His strength in the inner man.

A man who can master the challenges of the inner life will unquestionably have an influence on others.

Now that we are alert to the challenges that can come from *within* us, stay with me as we move on to the next chapter and look at some of the challenges that face us from *without*.

It is only the fear of God
that can deliver us from
the fear of man.[17]
—JOHN WITHERSPOON

6

Accepting the Challenge to Live Boldly

Be strong in the Lord,
and in the strength of His might.
—Ephesians 6:10 (NASB)

Have you ever tried to define *obedience?* That's the challenge a missionary ran up against as he was translating the Bible. Taking a break from his search for a meaning, he called to his dog. When the dog came running, a tribal observer said, "Your dog was all ear." Instantly the missionary had the words he needed to define *obedience*—"to be all ear."

I'm sure by now you've noticed obedience is a key element in becoming a man of influence. And, in the previous chapter, we learned about the challenges of ignorance, the flesh, and apathy. Let's continue on with our list of challenges that a man faces every day. And as we do so, let's aim at accepting God's challenge to live in *bold* obedience—to be all ear!

The Challenges of Obedience

The challenge of fear—One of the biggest challenges you and I face in our obedience to God is the fear of reprisal—fear of the consequences of doing the right thing. Ananias was afraid of what Paul had done to Christians and of what Paul might do to him. Ananias's fear tempted him to waver in his obedience to God's desire to use him as a man of influence and impact.

The challenge of this type of fear is not limited to Ananias or you or me. (And don't say you are never challenged with fear!) Even the great apostle Paul had his bouts with fear. For instance, Paul's path of obedience to God ultimately led him through Macedonia to the great cities of Athens and Corinth (Acts 17–18). Both of these cities were very large...and very decadent.

Corinth was especially worldly and immoral. This great city housed the temple of Aphrodite, the goddess of love, with its 1,000 priestess-prostitutes. In the ancient world of Paul's day, Corinth was noted for everything sinful. Referring back to his initial visit to this corrupt city, Paul later wrote to the Corinthians that his exposure to them and their city was actually "in weakness and *fear*, and with much trembling" (1 Corinthians 2:3). All men of influence experience fear at some time or other. And here's another fact: fear usually comes when we are in a hostile environment and must stand up for our faith.

While you and I are not being asked to walk into a sinful place like Corinth, we *are* being asked to stand up and speak up for the Christian faith and Christian values in the midst of an antagonistic workplace or at our child's school. We are confronted with the sinfulness of our society not on an irregular basis, but daily! And if you're anything like me, you are not immune to fear when those situations occur.

But the issue is not our fear. Fear is normal. No, the issue is our *response* to fear. Fear can immobilize us, or fear can be used as a bridge to power—God's power that can work in us. Paul explains from his own life how he asked the Lord three times to take away a mysterious "thorn in my flesh." And what was God's answer? "My grace is sufficient for you, for my power is made perfect in weakness" (2 Corinthians 12:8). God empowered Paul in his fears and weaknesses to face the challenges in his life.

The next time you and I should stand up for Christ and fear starts welling up, we need to first recognize we're too weak to handle the situation alone. Then we need to pray that God would override our fears so that whenever we open our mouths, words may be given to us so we "will *fearlessly* make known the mystery of the gospel" (Ephesians 6:19).

The challenge of peer pressure—Peer pressure is the twin sister of fear. Peer pressure creates a fear not of our enemies and hostile situations, but of our family, friends, workmates, and neighbors—our peers. We're afraid that others will laugh at us, or reject us, or torment us if we stand up for our faith and God's standards.

If you think you're the only one who has struggled with this challenge, think again. Read below how peer pressure in all its power affected the great apostle Peter and even Paul's close friend Barnabas. Paul reports,

> When Peter came to Antioch, I opposed him to his face, because he was clearly in the wrong. Before certain men came from James, he used to eat with the Gentiles. But when they arrived, he began to draw back and separate himself from the Gentiles because he was *afraid* of those who belonged to the circumcision group. The other Jews joined him in his hypocrisy, so that by their hypocrisy even Barnabas was led astray (Galatians 2:11-13).

In short, these two men, men who were supposed to be men of influence, had caved in to peer pressure.

Does this sound familiar? I know it does for me. I know I've caved in at one time or another when I allowed peer pressure to overrule what I knew to be God's standard. And I'm sure you're aware that every day you must decide, Will I follow the crowd,

or will I boldly follow Christ? You cannot follow both! So...
which will it be?

Again, let's take Paul's cue on boldness in the face of peer
pressure. What did he do? Paul requested that others pray for
him so that whenever he opened his mouth, "words may be
given me so that I will *fearlessly* make known the mystery of the
gospel" (Ephesians 6:19).

Like Paul, be **B-O-L-D**.

B-e not afraid.

O-btain the prayer support of others.

L-ook to the Lord for His strength.

D-ecide daily to boldly follow Christ.

The challenge of our culture—Living a bold and godly life in
an ungodly culture is also a constant challenge. Any time you
and I stand up for what we believe, we will be challenged by our
culture—you can count on it! As Paul told his young disciple,
Timothy, "*Everyone* who wants to live a godly life in Christ
Jesus will be persecuted" (2 Timothy 3:12). Fellow Christian
man, when you signed on as a soldier of Jesus Christ, you
signed on to a life that is not to be "entangled with the affairs
of everyday life" (2 Timothy 2:3 NASB). You *live* in this world,
but you are not to *love* this world (1 John 2:15). Just because
some people cheat on their taxes or pad their expense accounts
or make "shady deals"—and just because such acts seem to be
culturally accepted—doesn't make it okay for you to do such
things. No, you and I are to live boldly by different standards—
God's standards!

Several months ago I came up against this challenge of culture. I was trying to sell a used boat trailer in the middle of
winter. (Do you know how hard it is to sell a boat trailer when
it's hardly 30 degrees outside and no one is boating?) Well, you
can imagine how thankful I was to the Lord when a potential
buyer contacted me. This man was even willing to pay my

asking price. The only catch was that he wanted me to put only half the worth of the trailer on the bill of sale. He said, "That's the way we do it in these parts." If I complied, he wouldn't have to pay but half the state sales tax, which amounted to several hundred dollars. I have to confess that my first thoughts were along these lines: *I really want to sell that trailer…but if I say no, he might back out…and I may not be able to find anyone else who will pay my asking price…but if I agree, then I will be lying (not to mention breaking the law!)…but who would know…?*

There I was, for the first few moments having this inner struggle, thinking all these terrible thoughts, knowing all the time what I should do, but still struggling! Well, brother, you will be glad to know that I refused his illicit offer. In fact, I told him boldly I was a Christian and that I didn't want to do anything illegal. I wanted to be obedient to God's standards, and I was prepared to lose the sale rather than go along with what was culturally acceptable in "these parts." (And, by the way, the man did pay me the full price, and I did declare the full amount on the bill of sale.)

While I didn't lose the sale, I was prepared to do so. And there will be times when you and I will "lose out" because we won't compromise. But, believe me, that "loss" is nothing compared to what is gained—God's blessing for our obedience, and a clear conscience for doing what is right.

Friend, you and I are called to live boldly and obediently by different standards—God's standards. That means you and I must…

- Find out God's standards.

- Make God's standards our standards.

- Determine to live by those standards.

- Be willing to accept the consequences of living by those standards.

- Be accountable to others for following God's standards.

- Pray for God's strength to boldly withstand the pressures to compromise God's standards.

Accepting the Challenges

I'm not much of a student of the laws of physics, but it doesn't take much of a student to understand that where there is no resistance, there is no pressure. And that same law could apply to our spiritual lives as well—where there is no resistance to sin (that is, when we disobey), there is no challenge to obedience. There are no challenges...

...when you allow fear to immobilize you

...when you allow peer pressure to compromise you

...when you allow your culture to conform you

...when you allow ignorance to stupify you

...when you allow apathy to pacify you

But I think better of you. I believe you are ready to accept the challenges that come with obedience. I believe you want your life to have a bold impact for God...and that you want to become a man of godly influence. With God's help (and that's what it will take) you are ready to be used in a powerful way by God.

Here then are a few suggestions that will definitely help you develop a life of influence and lasting impact. And forgive me if I repeat myself, but you and I can never be reminded enough of these simple steps!

Step 1: *Realize that God's Word is God's Word to you.* As an excuse for disobedience, some people say, "If God would speak to me in a vision like He did to Paul and Ananias, or like He did with Moses, then I would obey." But friend, God *has* revealed Himself to us! God has revealed Himself to us in His Son, Jesus Christ, and in His Word, the Bible. Let's stop making excuses and start obeying God's Word.

Step 2: *Realize what God's commands are and obey them.* What kind of commands? Commands like...

- "Husbands, love your wives" (Ephesians 5:25).

- "Whatever you do, work at it with all your heart, as working for the Lord, not for men" (Colossians 3:23).

- "Everyone must submit himself to the governing authorities" (Romans 13:1).

- "Each of you must put off falsehood and speak truthfully" (Ephesians 4:25).

- "Go and make disciples of all nations" (Matthew 28:19).

Step 3: *Constantly seek God's strength to follow through on His commands.* "Be strong in the Lord and in the strength of His might" (Ephesians 6:10 NASB). What God *expects* us to do, He also *enables* us to do. The strength comes from Him. We just need a willing heart.

Step 4: *Repent when you have disobeyed God's standards.* God is not asking you to be perfect, but He *is* asking you to progress and grow in maturity. God uses pure vessels. So...

...keep a clean slate with God,

...acknowledge your sin,

...accept the forgiveness God offers, and

...move on boldly for God.

Step 5: *Rejoice in even the smallest victories.* No war is ever won in one battle. And neither is our war against the challenge to obedience. Spiritual growth happens one step at a time, one victory at a time. So thank God even for the smallest of victories in Jesus Christ (Romans 7:24).

> Your outcome in life doesn't depend on
> your income, but on how
> you overcome.

As I've said before, it all comes down to this: *An influential life* for *God is dependent on an obedient life* to *God.*

We will never get anywhere in life
without discipline....
This is doubly so in spiritual matters.
None of us naturally seeks after God....
As children of grace, our spiritual discipline
is everything—everything!
I repeat...discipline is everything![18]

1

Pursuing Spiritual Discipline

Train yourself to be godly.
—1 TIMOTHY 4:7

I'm sure you've heard and probably read many inspiring stories about those who have overcome great adversity and overwhelming odds to compete in the Olympics or some other world-class sports event. One such story that has inspired and challenged me is that of Lance Armstrong.

Lance has won (at the time of this writing) four first-place finishes in the grueling 2,000-mile, three-week long Tour de France, the premiere event in cycling. What makes Lance's story so amazing is that he won his first title less than three years after being diagnosed with an advanced form of cancer that had spread to his lungs and brain. He was given a 40-percent chance of survival and underwent brain surgery and chemotherapy.

The very nature of Lance Armstrong's accomplishments has made him a man of influence. His life shows us what the human spirit can achieve with discipline, determination, and mental toughness (along with good doctors and the latest medicines). Lance is a world-class cyclist, and to reach this level of influence he has had to exert superhuman effort just to prepare himself to compete, not to mention to win in competition! His challenging life of discipline illustrates yet another of the secret inner qualities found in the lives of all men of influence—discipline.

The Focus on Discipline

As we have already witnessed, one man of major-league influence was the apostle Paul. And one of the reasons for Paul's great influence was that he was a disciplined man! There's no doubt about it. Like our cycling friend Lance, Paul was a competitor and highly motivated. Where, we might wonder, did he get his drive? Was it because of his strict religious training as a Pharisee? Was it what some people call a Type-A personality?

These elements may have contributed to Paul's drive, but the real reason for Paul's discipline was the focus of his life. Paul passionately and persistently focused on the "crown that will last forever" (1 Corinthians 9:25). Lance Armstrong, and others who compete at any level in any sports event or business venture, have their earthly reasons for their high levels of motivation—an earthly prize, a "crown that will not last." But Paul's motivation was Jesus Christ—an eternal prize. And brother, that focus made all the difference! Paul wanted to *pursue* the knowledge of Jesus Christ (Philippians 3:10). Paul wanted to *preach* the message of Jesus Christ (1 Corinthians 9:16). And Paul was willing to *pay any price* and do whatever it took to stay in the Christian race for Jesus Christ. As I said, Jesus Christ was the complete focus of Paul's life. And the more Jesus Christ influenced Paul, the more Paul influenced others.

Your Personal Passion

Paul's motivation to please Jesus Christ and to obtain an eternal prize were chief contributors to his life of discipline. These were his goals and his passion. And friend, like Paul, you and I have certain people or things who are driving our life. So I ask you, What is motivating you these days? What is getting you up early every morning and keeping you up late at night? What is consuming the hours and days of your life? Is it a career? Is it a desire for success? Is it the goal of financial independence? Is it a dream of future happiness or retirement?

These desires in and of themselves may not be wrong or evil. But what happens when you reach any of these physical or financial goals, these "earthly" prizes? Will you be satisfied? Maybe. But also maybe not. My friend, here's the hard question: Are you willing to take a chance and expend your life and energies on these kinds of pursuits that, in the end, might *not* fulfill your deepest longings? While you're thinking about your answer, read on.

Paul's Personal Passion

I hope you're learning a lot about the apostle Paul. This man's life-study has become a passionate lifetime pursuit for me. And now we're going to look at yet another way he can school us toward becoming men of influence.

Paul was a man who had it all. He had the right background, the right job, and was the best at what he did. He was making excellent progress toward the top of his "profession." But after he became a Christian, Paul saw his accomplishments and goals in a different light. So he gave up all his earthly and personal pursuits for something better—far better! He gave all of it up for a life of following hard after Jesus Christ. Hear the heart of Paul as he searches for the words to describe for us the new focus of his life:

> Whatever was to my profit I now consider loss for the sake of Christ. What is more, I consider everything a loss compared to the surpassing greatness of knowing Christ Jesus my Lord, for whose sake I have lost all things. I consider them rubbish, that I may gain Christ (Philippians 3:7-8).

My friend, discipline is a good and profitable thing. You will never get anywhere without it. You will never be a man of influence on any level without discipline. But make sure your discipline has the right focus, the right direction. Like Paul, make sure your goal is, first and foremost, Jesus Christ. Then all else will fall into place. In fact, that's what Jesus Himself said: "Seek first the kingdom of God and His righteousness and all these things [the necessities of life] shall be added to you" (Matthew 6:33 NKJV).

As you can see from Christ's words, discipline for the Christian man is really *spiritual* discipline. As we put our time and energy into our spiritual life, God replaces old destructive habits and thoughts with godly habits and God-honoring thoughts and desires.

Lance Armstrong and others like him most definitely have positions of influence in life and society, and we want to acknowledge their noteworthy accomplishments and learn from them. But true and lasting influence comes from living our lives for Jesus Christ, as Paul discovered. Such a God-honoring life has the greatest kind of influence on others. Therefore we have to ask the obvious question: How do we get this kind of life? This is where spiritual discipline comes in.

The Characteristics of Spiritual Discipline

Paul gives us a simple description of spiritual discipline in a letter to his young disciple Timothy: *Train yourself to be godly.* From this simple-but-profound admonition to Timothy (found in 1 Timothy 4:7) we can discern three characteristics of spiritual discipline.

1. *Spiritual discipline is demanding*—"*Train* yourself to be godly." This act of "training" is also translated "discipline" (NASB) and "exercise" (KJV), issuing to us the command to constantly discipline ourselves to be godly. The word "train" speaks of the rigorous, strenuous, self-sacrificing training a good athlete

undergoes.[19] Therefore, my friend, Paul is urging you and me, as he urged his protégé Timothy, to continually and rigorously pursue a life of godly discipline. And, just as an athlete cannot afford to take a day off in his physical training without suffering a physical setback, neither can you or I afford to take time off from our spiritual discipline...even though the cost of spiritual discipline is great and very demanding.

I have experienced two vocational moves in my life. The first involved moving out of the pharmaceutical profession and into full-time ministry. As you might imagine, my spiritual growth was greatly accelerated by my involvement in ministry and the time such ministry requires in spiritual pursuits and preparations. The second move came several years ago when I moved out of "professional ministry" and into a writing and speaking ministry. With the second move I incorrectly assumed that, because I was researching and writing and speaking about spiritual things, I didn't need to spend as much of my personal time pursuing spiritual disciplines such as reading my Bible and praying.

Things were fine for a while...until I, along with my wife, began to notice some ungodly behavior beginning to creep in—behavior such as impatience, irritability, and even hints of anger. The changes were so subtle! And all due to a seemingly small thing, like failing to read my Bible regularly for my own spiritual growth. But the cost to my spiritual life was great! Friend, take it from me: Spiritual discipline is demanding, and must be a constant pursuit!

2. *Spiritual discipline must be desired*—Look at Paul's words again. But this time, catch a different message as you focus on a different word. He said, "Train *yourself* to be godly." Brother, this is not a suggestion! Godliness is not optional. No, God desires that you and I, as His men, along with Paul and Timothy, be conformed to the image of His Son (Romans 8:29). This desire must be at the very heart of our being. This hunger for self-disciplined training in the ways of God must go beyond

the wishing stage and become reality as we actually do something about spiritual discipline.

I don't know about you, but I know that if I want to stay healthy, I should do something about my body every day. I need to participate in some form of physical exercise. My head says *yes*, but my heart and body say *no*. (And you can guess which part of me usually wins!) Well, this same scenario plays out in the spiritual realm. My head says *yes*, but my flesh says, *Let's do something spiritual some other time.*

The truth is that in both the physical and the spiritual realms of a man's life, the only way to make the "workout" a reality is by an act of the will. Ultimately, I have to decide to get up from my couch and go do some physical exercise. And the same is required in my spiritual life. Ultimately, I have to decide to get up from my couch and go pick up my Bible.

So how can we move forward on our desire to become men of tremendous influence? Answer: Ask God to give you a greater desire to grow spiritually. (And while you're at it, ask Him to help you get up off *your* couch and do something physically healthy!)

3. *Spiritual discipline points toward God*—Once again, let's consider Paul's words to Timothy (and us), but this time with a different emphasis: "Train yourself *to be godly.*" *Godliness* is at the center of the Christian life. Therefore, godliness should be the direction of every believer's life. What is godliness? I believe this definition goes straight to the heart of what it means:

> Godliness is a right attitude and response toward the true Creator God; a preoccupation from the heart with holy and sacred realities. It is respect for what is due to God, and is thus the highest of all virtues.[20]

If you and I are God's children, then we should want to be like God as much as is humanly possible. But our sinful flesh resists this goal. Even the great apostle Paul struggled in this area. Hear again...and sense again...his constant battle:

> So I find this law at work: When I want to do good, evil is right there with me. For in my inner being I delight in God's law; but I see another law at work in the members of my body, waging war against the law of my mind and making me a prisoner of the law of sin at work within my members. What a wretched man I am! Who will rescue me from this body of death? (Romans 7:21-24).

I sure can identify with Paul's anguish! You probably can too. But, my friend, there's hope! Paul gives us the answer to both his struggle and ours. You can almost hear him shout, "Thanks be to God—through Jesus Christ our Lord!... because through Christ Jesus the law of the Spirit of life set me free from the law of sin and death" (Romans 7:25; 8:2).

Jesus Christ has set us free to willfully and joyously serve Him and pursue His godly nature. So, as men who love the Lord and desire to influence others to do the same, let's point our spiritual compass toward home...toward God...toward eternity.

The Value of Spiritual Discipline

Maybe you're reading along and thinking, *Why is this so important? Why go to all this trouble? What's the value?* Well, Paul must have known you would ask those questions, for he now tells us the value of spiritual discipline in a word—godliness: *"Physical training is of some value, but godliness has value for all things, holding promise for both the present life and the life to come"* (1 Timothy 4:8).

There's not a man reading this book who wouldn't agree that physical training has value—right? We know that physical exercise is beneficial for us. Paul agrees: Go join a gym. Start walking. Lose a few pounds.

But don't stop with training just the physical realm, which has "some value." If you want what will *really* count, what will have a *lasting* impact, then put your main focus on your spiritual life. This will help you enjoy the best of both worlds. Spiritual discipline will help you in your present life—your marriage, your children, your job, your ministry, your testimony—and in your future life as well. Now that's value!

I hope you understand why spiritual discipline is such an important part of becoming a man of influence. Spiritual maturity is a necessary element in the life of God's man. With that in mind, in the next chapter we will look at the steps you and I need to take to become more disciplined spiritually. But first, think through this challenge:

> You no more need a day off from spiritual concentration on matters in your life than your heart needs a day off from beating. As you cannot take a day off morally and remain moral, neither can you take a day off spiritually and remain spiritual. God wants you to be entirely His, and it requires paying close attention to keep yourself fit. It also takes a tremendous amount of time.[21]

The world is full of naturally brilliant people
who never rise above mediocrity
because they will not make the sacrifice
which superiority requires.[22]

Without discipline we are not disciples,
even though we profess His name and
pass for a follower of the lowly Nazarene.
In an undisciplined age when liberty and licenses
have replaced law and loyalty,
there is greater need than ever before
that we be disciplined to be His disciples.[23]

8

PRACTICING PERSONAL DISCIPLINE

I beat my body and make it my slave so that...
I myself will not be disqualified for the prize.
—1 CORINTHIANS 9:27

There have been many men who have influenced my life, but three men in particular have made a lasting impact.

First there was my father. My dad modeled a number of basic areas of discipline for me. He taught me the value of hard work, the need for thrift, and the reward of providing for your family. I owe a lot to my father's example and his many fatherly reminders about the importance of discipline.

Next was my scoutmaster. Mike was a successful executive at a local company. He had four girls, and I think he wished he had had a boy or two! So he went out into my neighborhood and recruited a group of little guys to form a scout pack and a basketball team. Mike taught us the discipline of working together as a team, whether we were pitching a tent in the woods or playing basketball. Every time I serve on a committee or tie a square knot, I think of Mike.

Then there was my pastor of more than 25 years, John MacArthur. John drilled into me the value of disciplined Bible study, the importance of interpreting the Bible correctly, and a deep respect for the Word of God and its transforming power in a man's life.

Each of these men had a marked influence on my life. Each chiseled some facet of discipline into my life and character. Each man, too, in his own way and in his own sphere, is and was a man of influence. Each had or has had a lasting impact on others—my father on me, Mike on a rag-tag bunch of neighborhood boys, and John MacArthur on a church congregation and the world through his audiotapes and books.

The Journey Toward Discipline

It's been said that a journey of a thousand miles begins with a single step. Well, the journey toward spiritual discipline (and becoming a man of influence) begins with a few first steps toward God. Let me share with you what those steps are.

Step 1: *Determine to become more disciplined*—If nothing I have said so far has motivated you to become more disciplined, then ponder the end result of strolling through life as an undisciplined person. Imagine the disappointment you will be to yourself, to God, and to your family if you fail to be the man you could have been simply because you didn't make the effort, because you took the easy road.

I'm sure you have heard the slogan "No pain, no gain." That slogan is usually posted in a gym or over a locker room door. But these same four words are also a perfect paraphrase of the personal philosophy of achievement of our man-of-influence, Paul. He said, "I beat my body and make it my slave so that...I myself will not be disqualified for the prize" (1 Corinthians 9:27). Discipline, whether in the spiritual or the physical realm, requires effort. But the effort is well worth it. You will receive a double prize—the eternal prize that Paul is talking about, and the earthly prize of accomplishment and influence.

Why not determine today that, with God's help, you want to emerge as a man of influence, as one who practices personal discipline as a lifestyle? Determine today that *you* will apply greater energy to the different roles that are required of *you*—

your role as the spiritual head of your family, your role as a husband, father, provider, friend, and even son and son-in-law. Godly influence doesn't just happen without any effort. Discipline in any area of your life starts with desire. It takes time to develop the disciplines required for spiritual maturity and personal accomplishment, and it all starts with desire. And it starts today.

What is the level of your desire?

What you are tomorrow, you are becoming today.

Step 2: *Develop spiritual sensitivity*—What does spiritual sensitivity mean? It means to walk through life with a God-consciousness. To be spiritually sensitive, we need to know how God would act, talk, and respond to life's situations. So how can you and I develop this kind of sensitivity?

One way is to read about God in the Bible. There, He has written to us about Himself. As we read the Bible, we begin to understand the nature and character of God. As we see how He responded graciously to His fallen creation and sacrificed His only Son for us, we begin to understand how we should be more loving, giving, and sacrificial. As we become more sensitive to spiritual truths, we become more discerning about the everyday issues we face in life.

Spiritual sensitivity means that you and I are always asking, "How would Jesus respond to this situation or to this person?" Paul called this "having [the] attitude in yourselves which was also in Christ Jesus" (Philippians 2:5). So now the question becomes this: How do we develop this attitude or mind of Christ?

Years ago a great man of God named Harold Lindsell came to our church to conduct a seminar. Dr. Lindsell was a professor and author and had done much in his earlier days to defend the Christian faith against liberal thinking. It was quite evident throughout the one-day seminar that he really knew his Bible.

After the seminar I summoned up my courage, went to him, and asked how he came to know the Bible so well. I expected him to say it was his theological training or his ability to interpret Scripture. But, to my surprise, he said it was *a lifetime of regularly and systematically reading through the Bible that gave him his depth of understanding of God's Word.* That's pretty simple, isn't it? What a joy it was to realize that I, too, could have a solid grasp of God's Word! All it would take was the discipline of being faithful to read my Bible.

Brother, that seminar with Dr. Harold Lindsell lasted for only one day. But his influence produced a lifelong impact on me. Following his example, I have attempted to regularly read through God's Word for the past 25 years. (Does this story of my encounter with Dr. Lindsell help you better recognize the power of influence?)

Now, how are you doing in this area of your life? Are you disciplined? Are you consistent in your reading and studying of God's Word?

Spiritual sensitivity means you can
discern good from evil.

Step 3: *Improve your prayer life*—One evening while fulfilling my role as a deacon in my church, I met and interviewed a man and his wife for membership in our church. What a great couple! Well, one week later I was leading the prayer time for our Sunday school class and asked several different men to pray for the group's prayer requests. After the class was over, the man I had interviewed for membership came up to me. He was visibly shaken and pleaded with me to please never call on him to pray! He said he was not good at prayer.

Why is it so hard for some men to pray? Maybe the answer is as simple as this: We don't pray enough to feel comfortable praying with our wife and family or in a public meeting at church. Prayer, like any of the other spiritual disciplines, requires repetition.

(And, by the way, this man and I started meeting and praying together. Today, most people in the church would consider him to be a man of prayer, both in private and in public. You and I, like my hesitant friend, can learn to pray simply by praying. If you've felt awkward about praying, find someone who will help you learn to pray. That's what the disciples did— they asked Jesus to help them!)

"Lord, teach us to pray" (Luke 11:1).

Step 4: *Deal with your sin*—Remember our definition of *godliness* from the last chapter? Godliness is living like and for God. To do that we need to deal with our sin. *Sin* is a foreign word for most people today. Most will say, "I made a mistake," or "I committed an indiscretion." But to be a man of godly influence, you and I must recognize sin for what it is and confront it head on. Sin is anything that misses the mark, and that mark is the standard set by God Himself in His Word.

How can you be a proper influence on others if you don't deal with sin in your life? You can't. But as the Bible states, "If we confess our sins, he is faithful and just and will forgive us our sins and purify us from all unrighteousness" (1 John 1:9). Confession of sin opens up the way for us to be the right kind of influence. And it's when we deal with our sin that we are developing our spiritual sensitivity, learning to discern what is right and what isn't.

How can we know when we've sinned? In the Bible, God tells us how He wants us to live. You can see again why it's so important that we read our Bible. You will never know when you are missing God's mark without knowing the instructions in "God's Rule Book." The Bible contains and communicates God's standards for your life.

Deal with your sin...or God will.

Step 5: *Worship with God's people*—Your first priority as a Christian man is to your physical family. God holds you accountable for being the spiritual leader of your family. That may seem scary, but the good news is that your leadership can begin with the easy, do-able step of taking your family to church. You set a godly example and have a tremendous influence on your family just by getting your family involved in church. So start with just attending church!

But your influence shouldn't stop with church attendance. You also have a responsibility to your spiritual family or your church family, the body of Christ. You take your family to church to *worship God*, but you and I are also called to go to church to *serve God's people*. This service comes as we use our spiritual gifts. Spiritual gifts are God-given abilities that are entrusted to us at salvation and are to be used to minister to others in the church. First Corinthians 12:7 says each Christian's spiritual gifts are to be used "for the common good." We'll learn more in a later chapter about our service to the people of God. But for now, simply make it a habit to cultivate the spiritual discipline of worshiping with God's people each week in a local church and to look for opportunities for service. Your example of weekly worship with God's people will have a profound impact on others—starting with your family.

God created us to worship Him.

Discipline and a Life of Influence

Over the last few chapters we've learned the great value of discipline, and I trust you are sensing the importance of discipline in a man's life. Whether it's Lance Armstrong, the apostle

Paul, or the men who have influenced your life, the reason for their influence is their disciplined lifestyle. We could list and comment on many other spiritual disciplines that round out a man of discipline and influence—disciplines such as meditation, fasting, and giving tithes. But you've gotten a good start with the disciplines of reading your Bible, praying, dealing with sin, and attending church. Now we're going to move on and look at how discipline fleshes itself out in eight major areas of a man's life. But before we do, I'd like to share one final thought regarding discipline:

> While…failure may at times be due to limited ability, too often the deficiency is not in native endowment but in character. The capacity for grueling application is lacking. There may be the promising start, but not the discipline required to carry through. Even if by good fortune or "pull" the undisciplined man should reach the position of [influence], he cannot maintain it, for he is not inwardly prepared. He collapses under the weight of responsibility, and the pressure and complexity of detail. He lacks the strength of leadership, the fullness of knowledge, the soundness of judgment, which can only be built up bit by bit through years of painstaking toil.[24]

The Nature of Discipline

- Discipline is a spiritual issue—*everything* done to the glory of God (1 Corinthians 10:31).

- Discipline has no shortcuts—no quick results.

- Discipline has no reserve—self-control must be reinstituted tomorrow.

- Discipline begins with the little things—like your dirty socks.

- Discipline tackles the difficult thing—easy requires little.

- Discipline starts with the mind—"I will."

- Discipline proceeds with a mandate—"I must."

- Discipline never gets distracted—"This one thing I do."

- Discipline never takes a vacation—it's for life.

- Discipline is ever-changing—growth requires new disciplines to meet life's next and latest challenges.

The true value of your life and the extent of your influence will be dependent on how you develop your life, how you put the "raw material" to use. Goals can help you to live out the potential that God has placed in you.
—JIM GEORGE

9

DEVELOPING LIFELONG GOALS

It has always been my ambition
to preach the gospel where Christ was not known.
—ROMANS 15:20

Aspiration is a good thing for us as men. Do you remember, as a young boy, dreaming about becoming a fireman, a policeman, a great athlete, an astronaut, a scientist, or a fighter pilot (that was my dream!)? These dreams may or may not have been realized at this point in your life. But dreams are not just for the young. And they are certainly not just for one phase of our lives! No, no matter what our age or station, we still need to have a passion, a deep desire, a focus, a direction for our lives. We need to ask ourselves constantly, "Where am I going with my life? Am I living out the right priorities for my life? Are the things I'm doing today going to have a lasting impact on others?"

A key to answering these questions is understanding, as a Christian man, what it means to have godly ambition. You and I need to know what God is asking of each of us as a Christian man (and as a Christian husband if we are married, and as a Christian father if we have children, and so on). Once we know God's calling for us, we can set the right goals, which will help us develop a life of influence for the glory of God.

The Need For Godly Ambition

Ambition can be both positive and negative. I am sure you have been exposed to ambitious people who have scratched their way to the top and, in the process, have left their claw marks on the backs of you and others whom they have climbed over in order to reach their goal.

That's not the kind of ambition we want to talk about in this chapter! No, the kind of ambition we are talking about is a *godly* ambition. What do I mean by godly ambition? A godly ambition is a desire to serve God and to spend our life and energies fulfilling all His will (see God's comments about King David in Acts 13:22). A man of influence has goals and ambition, to be sure. But those goals and that ambition are not for himself. God's man strives solely for the glory of God and the good of others.

Paul is a perfect example of a man with godly ambition. From the day he received his commission from God to go to the Gentiles (Acts 22:21), he was relentless in his drive. But his drive had its focus in the will of God. Paul's focus is evident in his words, "I will come to you very soon, if the Lord is willing," and "I know that when I come to you, I will come in the full measure of the blessing of Christ" (1 Corinthians 4:19 and Romans 15:29).

Paul's ambition was to preach the gospel. Therefore he had recruited and trained others who eventually shared this goal, enabling his influence to spread to many regions. So when Paul wrote to his friends in Rome, he shared his desire to go to places where others had not yet gone. Why? Because he wanted to influence others with the gospel of Jesus Christ. He boldly penned, "It has always been my ambition to preach the gospel where Christ was not known" (Romans 15:20). In this case, the place Paul had in mind was Spain (Romans 15:24). The job of evangelism was getting done and God's will was being accomplished because Paul had lined up his ambition with God's calling for his life. In time, Paul desired to witness in Spain and to travel there by way of his friends in Rome.

Paul's example shows us that God's will, as mediated through our goals, can and should be a part of our life if we want to influence others. I believe this is part of what Paul had in mind when he said, "Follow my example, as I follow the example of Christ" (1 Corinthians 11:1). Let's follow Paul's example by bringing our ambition in line with God's will.

Some Benefits of Having Goals

What are your goals in life? Have you defined them yet? You'll find they can help you in a lot of ways. For example...

- *Goals give definition*—Goals change your thoughts from daydreams and make them concrete. Goals are statements about the future—what you believe might be the will of God for you. Goals can then bring that future (if the *Lord* wills...or if it is the Lord's *will!*) into the present so you can do something about God's future in your life today.

- *Goals give focus*—Men tend to stay busy doing so many little things that they don't have time to focus on the really big things and the important areas of life. But not Paul...or you! Paul stated in Philippians 3:13, "But *one* thing I do." Be sure your motto isn't "These *many* things I dabble in"!

- *Goals give motivation*—Goals are one of the most powerful motivational forces you can have in your life. They're what gets you out of bed at 5:00 A.M. They help excite and prod you along the way when you get weary. Read what one gentleman said about the motivational power of goals:

    Observing the lives of people who have mastered adversity, I have repeatedly noted that they have established goals and, irrespective of obstacles, sought with all their effort to achieve them. From the moment they've fixed an objective in their mind and decided to concentrate all their energies on a specific goal, they begin to surmount the most difficult odds.[25]

What a powerful force can be yours as you establish goals based on what you believe to be the will of God, and then allow the enabling power of the Holy Spirit to work through you as you serve God and others!

- *Goals help in the decision-making process*—How do you make your decisions? Without goals, your decisions are likely to be influenced by the demands of others, or made by default (no other option), or on the spur of the moment (you just can't seem to think of a good reason to say no). But with goals—goals based on God's will for your life—you will have a much better idea of how to make the best decisions.

- *Goals help develop your life and influence*—I once read about a Ripley's "Believe It or Not" article that pictured a plain bar of iron worth $5. The story went on to say that if the same bar of iron were made into horse shoes, it would be worth $50. If it were made into needles, the value would be $5000. If it were made into balance springs for fine Swiss watches, it would be worth $50,000. The point of the story was that raw material gains value according to how that raw material is developed.

Friend, God has created you and me in His image. That in itself settles our "worth" and our "value"! But we can still be a little rough around the edges, still in the "raw material" stage. However, we have the potential to develop. We develop our life and put the "raw material" to use. And goals can help in the process. Won't you accept the challenge to develop your life and influence?

Dear man of God, goals are important and should be a constant, ever-evolving part of what God is doing in your life. As a Christian man, are you seeking God's direction and setting goals in your life—goals for your work, your family, and your personal growth? I'm sure you've heard the popular saying, "Aim at nothing and you will hit it every time." Don't drift through life without a course, a compass, or a cause. Others are depending on your leadership. So take aim...set your goals... hit the target! Make a difference...and an impact! Make sure that when you die, people will know you were here.

Eight Areas of Life That Call for Goals

Once you and I understand that life is a "vapor" (James 4:14 NASB) and that soon we will be gone, determining our priorities becomes most urgent. Does that make you wonder what priorities you need to focus on? If so, I'm glad. Why? Because 97 percent of adults never write down their lifetime goals. Friend, I want you to be part of the 3 percent who do.

I believe you and I can streamline our priorities to eight major areas. We will start with two of the eight areas in this chapter, and finish the list over the next two chapters. And as we begin, I challenge you to prayerfully evaluate these eight areas of your life. Ask God to show you any weaknesses that need attention. And ask Him to show you the goals you need to set in these areas.

1. *Spiritual*—I'm sure you're thinking that I sound like a broken record. Well, maybe so. But your spiritual health is the key—the secret—to being a man of influence. As we learned earlier, this is the starting point for a life of influence. You cannot impart to others what you do not possess yourself. And the thing that is most important to impart to others is your vibrant, growing life in Christ.

You and I must also realize that spiritual growth is not optional. We are commanded in Scripture to grow in grace and knowledge (2 Peter 3:18). If you have started working on this area of your life, you might want to step up your efforts. Spiritual exercise, like physical exercise, must be continuous if we want to remain healthy. You can never live on past spirituality. Here are some ways you can "exercise" yourself toward greater spiritual growth:

- Read your Bible daily.

- Pray daily for your family and friends.

- Lead your family in prayer and devotions.

- Go to church regularly.

- Find someone to disciple you.

Are you concerned that taking the time to focus on these spiritual disciplines will cause some other areas of your life to suffer? That won't happen. Why? Because when you take care of your spiritual life, all the other parts of your life fall neatly into place. The famous writer C.S. Lewis observed, "Aim at heaven and you will get earth thrown in."

2. *Mental*—It's been said that the mind is a terrible thing to waste. Your mind is like your muscles. Use your muscles and you increase in strength. Use your mind and you increase in

your mental capabilities. I have heard statistics that say the average adult watches six hours of television a day. What a terrible waste! Watching that much television won't help us become men of influence. The Bible commands you to "be transformed by the renewing of your *mind*" so that you can know and do God's will (Romans 12:2).

How can you and I develop our mind? The best way is to *read.* I'm going to make a strong statement here and if you think about this carefully, I believe you'll find this to be true. *You will never be a leader in any area of your life if you are not a reader in those areas of life. You will never be a leader in your family, your job, your church, or your community if you are not a reader.* Brother, a reader is a leader...and a leader is a reader. It's as simple as that!

Why would I make such a strong statement? First, I have seen this happen in the lives of too many men to believe it's not true. And second, if you are not a reader and keeping yourself informed, you will tend to be more dependent on others to help you in certain matters or situations.

Now, some dependency is not bad, because all of us can benefit from those who are knowledgeable in certain areas—such as a pastor, who can teach us the Bible, or a banker, who can give us importan financial advice. But much of what others are eager to tell us is worldly and harmful, and can cause us to "conform" to the pattern of this world (Romans 12:2), as Paul said. But we're *not* to conform, but rather, to "be transformed by the renewing of your *mind*" (Romans 12:2). And the best way to renew our mind is to grow mentally as we feed upon the truths of God's Word.

When you are growing mentally, especially in the spiritual realm, your mind is being transformed. You are then "able to test and approve what God's will is" (Romans 12:2). You are steadily maturing and constantly training yourself to "distinguish good from evil" (Hebrews 5:14). This, in turn, will help you answer important questions, such as What is God's will for me and my family? What is good and what is evil?

Now, how can you become this man, this mental man of influence? Start by picking up a book—the Book, the Bible—and start reading. Next, pick out a book that deals with one of the eight major areas of life and start reading. Start learning. Start growing spiritually and mentally. Start having an impact. Start creating a life of godly influence and living a life of lasting impact. And as time goes on, you can read other books that can help you grow stronger in the eight areas we are studying in this and the next two chapters.

It concerns us to know the purposes we seek in life,
for then, like archers aiming at a definite mark,
we shall be more likely to attain what we want.
—ARISTOTLE

10

Defining Your Purpose

One thing I do:
Forgetting what is behind and
straining toward what is ahead,
I press on toward the goal....
—PHILIPPIANS 3:13-14

August 31, 1974 was a red-letter day in my life. Wow! That was the day my wife and I sat down together and each wrote some lifetime goals. Up until that day, I had flopped and floundered and made little or no progress in achieving much of anything with a lasting godly influence. Basically I had spent the first 30 years of my life drifting from one desire to another...and most of the time, without God in mind.

But then, on that life-changing Sunday afternoon, I decided I needed to ask God to give Elizabeth and me wisdom as we sat down to write goals—goals that we hoped would line up with His will for our lives. Today, almost 30 years later, both Elizabeth and I are still operating our lives according to those goals that were written with hearts full of hope—goals that have simplified our focus in life, goals that have allowed me to influence not only my wife and children, but also fellow believers in my church and the Christian community nationally and internationally.

Why are goals important to becoming a man of influence? Because they help us to define our purpose. For you and me as "heaven-born souls," we "cannot without great peril be content

97

to miss the smallest part of the Master's will"[26] and purpose for our lives. It's true that the poorest of all men is not the one without *gold*, but the one without a *goal*. As I learned from my own experience, life for a goalless man has no meaning and no purpose. There is little reason for living, and even littler impact! By contrast, goals give us direction, purpose, and help us know how to best use our time and energy—thus making us men of impact.

Eights Areas of Life That Call for Goals

In the previous chapter, we discussed two of the eight areas of life in which we ought to have goals—the *spiritual* and *mental* realms. Now let's "press on" and look at more areas in this chapter.

3. *Physical*—Vince Lombardi once said, "Fatigue makes cowards of us all." This legendary coach of the Green Bay Packers football team knew that "physical training is of some value" (1 Timothy 4:8). So did the apostle Paul. In fact, Paul wrote the words in 1 Timothy 4:8 regarding the value of physical training.

I'm sure you realize that people in America are known for being overindulgent in many ways...and that includes the physical realm. The average person in the United States is characterized as being 15 pounds overweight and in desperate need of exercise. However, as a man of influence, you must understand three truths:

—your body is a *stewardship* from God,

—your body is the *temple* of the Holy Spirit, and

—your body is meant to *glorify* God (1 Corinthians 6:19-20).

So how about a look in the mirror? How are you doing on your stewardship of God's temple, your body? Have you stepped on the scales today? When was the last time you did some physical exercise (other than walking to the refrigerator for another sandwich)? God cares about your body and health. Therefore you need to be careful about caring for yourself physically. Here are some suggestions (and notice that the first two deal with your spiritual life as well!):

- *Watch out for sin*—Psalm 32:3-5 tells us what happened to David's physical life when he failed to confess his sin. His body suffered, his bones wasted away, he suffered day and night, and his strength was sapped.

- *Walk by the Spirit*—One "fruit of the Spirit" you enjoy when you are walking in obedience to God's Word is "self-control" (Galatians 5:22-23). Self-control enables us to take better care of ourselves.

- *Weigh yourself every day*—If the arrow is pointing in the wrong direction, then go in the *right* direction by following the next suggestion.

- *Watch what you eat*—Paul said to "buffet" your body as in beat it—not "buffet" your body as in indulge yourself in a smorgasbord (1 Corinthians 9:27)! Watch both the quality and quantity of the food you take in (Daniel 1:12-15).

- *Work out regularly*—Get a little bit of physical training into your schedule—training that Paul said is of some value (1 Timothy 4:8).

- *Work at your stewardship*—You are not your own, and neither is your body. You were bought with a price—a high price!—by Jesus Christ. So be a good steward of it (1 Corinthians 6:19-20).

- *What you see is what you are*—Realize that your outward physical appearance reflects your inner spiritual condition. One picture is worth a thousand words! Do you like what you see?

- *Win the battle*—One of the apostle Paul's secrets to his life, his ministry, and his lasting impact is found in his battle cry regarding his body: "I...make it my slave" (1 Corinthians 9:27). Paul viewed his body as an opponent that had to be conquered at all costs...or else. Who's winning the battle for your body?

I have long followed the lives of leaders on every front, making the study of leadership a personal passion. In regard to the physical area, I particularly like what President Harry S. Truman, a no-nonsense politician from Missouri, observed: "In reading about the lives of great men, I found that the first victory they won was over themselves...self-discipline with all of them came first." A man of influence and a man of lasting impact is marked as a man of rigorous personal physical discipline. May you (and I) be such a man!

4. *Social*—Before you get the wrong idea, let me clarify that by using the word *social* I'm not talking about your party life. No, I'm talking about your relationships. You and I are in constant contact with people—at home, at work, at church, in the community...and the list goes on. If we want to have an influence on others, we need to be careful that we are not guilty of having too many of the wrong friends and not enough of the right friends. We are to be influencing people rather than being influenced by the wrong people.

Now the question is, How do you determine the level of importance of these contacts? What's more, we also need to prioritize our contacts in the right order. To make sure you are on the right track, realize that there are four different types or levels of people whom you are to influence.

Level 1: Your family—Next to your relationship with Jesus Christ, family is your top priority. Never sacrifice your relationship with your family for any lesser relationships. Christ said, "What will it profit a man if he gains the whole world and forfeits his soul?" (Matthew 16:26 NASB). When it comes to my family, I apply Christ's words in a slightly different way: "What will it profit a man to gain the whole world and lose his *family?*" My family is precious to me, and I work hard daily at making sure, even now when my children are grown and gone, that they are Number One.

Level 2: Your friends—Friends are a gift from the Lord. You should cultivate friendships with other men, especially other Christian men—men who will encourage you in your faith and give good advice. The Bible says, "As iron sharpens iron, so one man sharpens another" (Proverbs 27:17). And friend, that's the kind of *friends* you need. What does such a friendship look like? For a good study of brotherly love and friendship, Jonathan and David give us a model to follow (see 1 Samuel 18 and 20). These two men of influence…

> assented to the same authority,
>
> knew the same God,
>
> were going the same way,
>
> longed for the same things,
>
> dreamed mutual dreams,
>
> yearned for the same experiences
>
> of holiness and worship.[27]

When it comes to you and your friendships, I think it goes without saying (but I will say it anyway), that *you should be extremely cautious in your associations with any woman other than your wife.* A married man shouldn't maintain the kind of friendship with a woman that he might normally maintain with other men. The danger is too great that such a friendship will end up becoming more than that. The Bible says when a man is attracted to a woman other than his wife, he's "playing with fire" (Proverbs 6:27-29). And brother, you are bound to get burned!

Level 3: Your workmates—You work alongside others every day, and if you want to be a man of influence, you'll want to make an effort to build relationships with your workmates. The closer they get to you, the clearer they will see the image of Jesus Christ stamped on your life. Remember, no contact equals no impact! (And again, be careful in the level of your interaction with women at work.)

Level 4: Your encounters with neighbors and strangers—Be friendly with everyone you encounter. Give a smile, a word of encouragement, a helping hand. Show them the love of Christ. Be a good neighbor. The same is true for neighbors as for workmates—no contact equals no impact.

When it comes to your social life, be willing to go to the ends of the earth, if needed, to find those relationships that will either "pull you along" or "pull you up." And conversely, avoid at all costs (and like the proverbial plague!) anyone who would "pull you down" (1 Corinthians 15:33).

5. *Vocational*—In the book of Genesis we learn about the beginning of everything...including work. We read that "the LORD God took the man and put him in the Garden of Eden to *work* it and take care of it" (Genesis 2:15). Do you realize this scene took place before the Fall of mankind to sin? That

means that, contrary to popular belief, work is not a part of the curse. God did say after man's fall that our work would be more difficult, but God still wants you and me, as His men, to work and glorify Him (1 Corinthians 10:31). How can you, a man of influence, glorify God in your work?

- By providing for your family (1 Timothy 5:8).

- By seeing your job as a calling from God (Genesis 2:15).

- By striving for excellence (Colossians 3:23-24).

- By being content (1 Timothy 6:8).

- By submitting to your employer (Ephesians 6:5-8).

- By being a servant to others (Galatians 5:13).

- By being a good testimony with your life (2 Corinthians 3:2).

The quality of your influence is determined by the quality of your work. Therefore, my friend, do your work "with all your heart," as if you were "working for the Lord" (Colossians 3:23).

Defining Your Purpose

Yes, August 31, 1974 was a red-letter day for me. It sent my life into warp speed…and in the right direction. And things have never slowed down. Not for one second! Why? Because, for the first time in my life, I had a purpose that went beyond me—way beyond me. The goals I wrote took me from being a receiver to being a resource. You see, in the past, my selfish desires were just that—selfish. But as I began to plan my life for the glory of God and according to His Word, I saw myself as one who could help others and be a resource for God in their lives.

Now, I must ask you: What is your purpose? Have you written some goals that would define your purpose? If not, it's never too late to start. Defining your purpose through goal-setting will give your life new purpose that God can use.

Before we move on to the next chapter and look at more areas of our lives for which we should develop goals, I want to encourage you with this list of benefits we can enjoy when we set goals.

- Goals help define the purpose of your life.

- Goals help develop a streamlined life.

- Goals help determine a focus for your life.

- Goals help drive each day of your life.

- Goals help display the stewardship of your life.

- Goals help design a life of influence.

Where do you want to go in life?
How do you want to get there?
Do the roles you fill contribute to your goal?
What is really important that you do?
What merely fills up time?
In determining your best roles, keep those that
advance you toward your goal and
eliminate those that are useless and a drag.
Your trouble may be too many good roles.
You cannot afford to take on
more than you can handle well.[28]

Practicing God's Plan

Do your best to present yourself to God
as one approved, a workman who
does not need not be ashamed.
—2 TIMOTHY 2:15

It lasted only two hours, but when it was over, I had a golden set of goals for my life! I'm talking about that red-letter day I described in the last chapter. Well, writing the goals was the easy part. Next followed 30 years of practicing them! As I mentioned in the previous chapter, goals require a stewardship. Once I put on paper what I believed God was doing in my life as well as what He wanted me to do (and what I dreamed of doing for Him), I was then duty-bound to fulfill that stewardship. I, like Timothy in the scripture quote above, was being challenged to present myself to God as a steward of the life He had given me.

My heart's desire is to be a workman who will not be ashamed when I stand before my Lord someday—and I'm sure you feel the same way. And then I wonder, *How can I do my best to be that approved workman?* I think asking this question is a good first step for both of us. Once we have an answer, we can then take the next step and develop goals that reflect this desire to be an approved workman. And finally, we can then follow through and practice God's plan.

All that will become possible when we know the areas of our lives in which we need to develop goals. So far we have covered the spiritual, mental, physical, social, and vocational areas of our lives. Now let's look at the last three areas: financial, family, and ministry. And remember, as important as it is to have an understanding of God's plan for your life through goals, it's equally important that you live out God's plan on a daily basis. That's a central secret to living a life of influence!

Eight Areas of Life That Call for Goals

6. *Financial*—Do you remember I had said my father taught me about thrift? He also taught me how to manage the money I earned. He and I made a deal with these terms: Whatever I saved out of the weekly paychecks I earned while working during my high school years, he would match. What a deal! Believe me, I got in the habit of working hard, going to the bank each week, and depositing a certain portion of my hard-earned money into my savings account. Then, at regular intervals, Dad would add his portion. It was my first-ever "matching funds" program. Dad trained me to save...and he trained me well.

But I haven't said anything yet about my wonderful Christian mother, who also had a great impact on my life. Whereas my dad taught me how to save, my mother taught me how to give. She would often quote Jesus' words, "Where your treasure is, there your heart will be also" (Matthew 6:21). The motto of her life was, "You can't outgive God!"

I'm sure it's no surprise to you that we live in a very materialistic society. And if you and I are not careful, we can get caught up in the selfishness of materialism. The best way to blunt this curse of our culture is to practice the twin disciplines of saving and giving. Both disciplines benefit other people, and not ourselves.

These two disciplines—saving and giving—have served me well over the years. By having money set aside in a savings account, my family and I are prepared for uncertain times. (Believe me, we've had to dip into the savings during many an uncertain time!) And by giving sacrificially to God's causes, I'm helping others today and storing up treasures in heaven (Matthew 6:20).

Here now are five key suggestions for handling your finances. And notice the spiritual thread that intertwines even your financial life.

Balance—The writer of Proverbs 30:8-9 asked God to give him "neither poverty nor riches, but give me only my daily bread." Why? Because "otherwise, I may have too much and disown you and say, 'Who is the LORD?' Or I may become poor and steal, and so dishonor the name of my God." Not too little and not too much. Now, that's having a balance perspective on our own finances.

Trust—One of my biggest problems (and I'm sure you can identify) is trust. I wonder, *Can I trust God with my life and my finances?* Jesus gives us the answer: "Do not worry about your life, what you will eat or drink; or about your body, what you will wear" (Matthew 6:25). The writer of Proverbs adds this admonition: "Trust in the LORD with all your heart and lean not on your own understanding" (Proverbs 3:5). Friend, you can trust the Creator of all things with your finances!

Maturity—What if I said that your checkbook reveals your heart? That the way you handle your money is an indicator of your focus and spiritual maturity? Well, it's true! So take a look at your checkbook or credit card statement. What does it show? Large amounts of money spent on your pleasures, hobbies, and personal things? Or large amounts of money given to God for His work? It's been said that the difference between a boy and a man is the size and the price of his toys. Always remember that...

—How you use your finances reveals who you serve.

—"No one can serve two masters" (Matthew 6:24).

—"You cannot serve both God and Money" (Matthew 6:24).

—The focus of your finances reveals your heart (Matthew 6:21).

In fact, if you really stop and think about it, the money you have is not even your money! It's *God's* money, and you and I are simply *stewards* of His money. When we get to the point where we see ourselves as stewards of God's money, then we are gaining maturity in this difficult area of life.

Contentment—When it comes to our finances, we need to follow Paul's example. He was able to say, "I have learned the secret of being content in any and every situation" (Philippians 4:12). Try saying *no* to yourself in the "things" department. Try being content with what you have. Try being happy about what other people have. Try being content with "food and clothing" (1 Timothy 6:8). Try being content with "godliness" (verse 6). Now *that*, my friend, is "great gain," in both the financial department *and* in the spiritual department (verse 8)!

Budgeting—When you make and keep a budget, you are exercising "self-control," a fruit of the Spirit (Galatians 5:22). A budget is a battle plan for curbing the lure of our needs-driven society. A budget helps you see clearly how to properly manage God's resources. Ask any financial advisor what the first step to financial freedom is. I would be greatly surprised if you don't hear, "Make a budget... and keep it!"

7. *Family*—Earlier I commented on the fact that your number-one priority, after your relationship with God, is your relationship with your family. And if you are married, *it starts with your wife*. If you focus your love and attention on her, all other family relationships will fall into place. And your relationship with your wife starts with your relationship with God, who is your Ultimate Priority. If you have a vibrant, growing relationship with God, you will have the Spirit's love to give in building a vibrant, growing relationship with your wife. Your love for God will overflow in love for your wife. When you love God, your love for your wife and family will come naturally as well—what a bargain!

How do we demonstrate God's love? You and I need to do something every day to show our love. It doesn't have to be much. Little things go a long way. If your relationship with your wife is anything like mine, any bit of initiative will be appreciated. Here are two surefire suggestions to get you started.

First, *plan a date night each week*. Get a babysitter and go to a local fast-food place and spend an hour or two talking over the week, planning the future, catching up on how you are each living out God's plan for your lives, and dreaming big dreams together. And if you really want to make a good impression...

Second, *volunteer to babysit the kids* while your wife goes shopping or takes a class at the church or a local college.

I can't tell you the number of men I know who have been highly successful in their jobs and have, in their retirement years, been remorseful that they neglected their wife and kids along the way up the corporate ladder. Start by not sacrificing your relationship with your wife on the altar of corporate success. Then follow that up with a commitment to your children. If you are going to parent children, then you must shoulder the responsibility of being a godly, caring, seriously involved parent—a father who desires to be a godly influence.

And speaking of fatherly influence, Theodore Epp, the famed broadcaster from the Back to the Bible radio program, often said, "The one man who had the greatest effect on my life was my father. He taught me the necessity of absolute dependence on Christ for a useful Christian life." And then there is George Beverly Shea, the great soloist who sings at the Billy Graham crusades, who credits the spiritual counseling of his father as the greatest single influence on his life.

Fellow husband and father (and grandfather, if you have grandchildren), you can retire rich and still be the poorest man on earth if you have lost your family in the process. So watch out! Keep your God-given priorities in focus—God...then your wife...then your children. And don't forget your parents, to honor them as well (Ephesians 6:2). It's never too late to begin living out God's plans for you. If you haven't been the kind of husband and father we've been talking about, then start today. Set some goals to be God's loving husband and God's caring and influential father. Then be faithful to follow through and live out God's plan for you and your family.

8. *Ministry*—What does a godly man do? He serves! That's what the godly men of influence did in Acts 6:1-6. In the early church there was a need to provide food for the widows, so godly men—men "full of the Spirit and wisdom"—were appointed to take care of the physical needs of these widows.

The same kind of service is to be true of you and me. As believers in Christ, we have been spiritually re-created by God to serve Him and His people. The Bible calls our service "good works" (Ephesians 2:10), and we are expected to serve other members of the church, the body of Christ (Galatians 6:10). The good news is that service and good works is a ministry you can have today, right now. You need no training to be a servant. So *serve!*

But beyond the good works of physical service, we as men of God are also called to discover and use, for the good of the church, what the Bible calls "spiritual gifts" (1 Corinthians 12:1-7). These "gifts" are spiritual enablements given to Christians through the ministry of the Holy Spirit (verse 7).

How can you know what your spiritual gifts are?

- *Ask God about your spiritual gifts*—Ask Him for wisdom as you seek to serve.

- *Ask to serve*—Begin by serving. Serve anyone and everyone! Be faithful, and be growing spiritually. As you serve in ministry, you will discover your areas of giftedness. Like physical talents and abilities, spiritual gifts are discerned and developed as they are being used.

- *Ask others about your spiritual gifts*—What are others seeing as the fruit of your ministry? Don't be afraid to ask others.

- *Ask yourself about your spiritual gifts*—What are the areas of service that you enjoy most? Which avenue of service brings the greatest blessing to others?

As I review what I've written about the eight areas of our life that ought to have goals, I can't help but think of a teaching from the ancient Greeks. They were concerned with the development of "the whole man." They saw a man as less than whole if any part of the body, soul, or spirit was undeveloped. I think we can safely say that setting goals and practicing God's plan for these eight areas will make you not only a whole man, but a man of influence and lasting impact.

Setting Goals for Your Life

Well, friend (and here I am, saying it again!), sitting down on that Sunday afternoon and starting to develop a life of focus with a handful of goals was truly a turning point in my life. I shudder to think what the past 30 years might have been like without them! If you don't already manage your daily life with the help of some lifetime goals, I pray that you will do what I did. As a former pharmacist, here's my prescription for you:

℞   Pray and seek God's guidance.

℞   Set your goals.

℞   Review them often.

℞   Focus on them daily.

I guarantee that setting goals for your life and practicing them will benefit you and everyone you know. Your influence will be greatly enhanced if you do. This has been true for me and I've seen it in the lives of others. Setting and following such goals will, by God's grace, add up to a life of influence.

Now, I ask you...

> *What kind of leadership influence can you have on others, if you don't first know where you are going? A man of influence knows where he is going and how to get there. And others will gladly follow him there.*

You live in a world awash with sensual images
available twenty-four hours a day....
But God offers you freedom from the slavery of sin
through the cross of Christ, and
He created your eyes and mind with an ability
to be trained and controlled.
We simply have to stand up and
walk by His power in the right path.[29]

DEALING WITH TEMPTATION

No temptation has seized you
except what is common to man.
And God is faithful; he will not let you be tempted
beyond what you can bear. But when you are tempted,
he will also provide a way out
so that you can stand up under it.

—1 CORINTHIANS 10:13

Meet Augustine, a man who lived during the decline of the Roman Empire (A.D. 354–430). He was the Bishop of Hippo in northern Africa. Augustine contributed much to our understanding of the theology of the New Testament and is considered to be one of the greatest and most influential leaders in all of church history.

Now, Augustine was not always a man of godly influence. Like Paul, Augustine had a past. But unlike Paul, Augustine's past was sordid and littered with sensuality, immorality, and religious skepticism. His life of dissipation and pleasure was taking him nowhere, and his influence on others was purely negative.

Like the apostle Paul, Augustine had a dramatic conversion. And like Paul, Augustine experienced a complete reversal in his life's direction. But here's the difference: Paul turned from the life of a prideful religious Pharisee to a life of humility and faithful service for the cause of Jesus Christ. Augustine, however, turned from being a "womanizer" and a pleasure-seeker to a life of ministry, becoming one of the great defenders of the orthodox Christian faith.

Augustine's personal experience with sin and God's great grace lent intensity and realism to his writings, so much so that readers more than a thousand years later (such as Martin Luther, the driving force of the Protestant Reformation) were deeply impacted. His life reversal and subsequent victorious Christian life illustrates yet another secret and important quality in the life of a man of influence—he deals with temptation.

Two Men, Two Choices, Two Paths

There are a myriad of thoughts penned on the importance of choices. You've probably heard this one—

> Little choices determine habit;
> Habit carves and molds character
> Which makes the big decisions.

Or how about this one?: "Choice, not chance, determines human destiny."

To see these truths lived out, meet two men...who made two choices...that led to two paths and two destinies.

Cain—Man #1 was Cain, the firstborn son of Adam and Eve. Cain and his brother Abel brought gifts to God, and their gifts received two different responses from God. Abel and his gift were pleasing to God, but Cain and his gift were not (Genesis 4:1-8).

What happened when God judged against Cain's gift? Cain had two choices for his response—he could either come before God and humbly ask forgiveness for himself and the nature of his gift, or he could become angry with God because of the rejection. Unfortunately, Cain chose the latter, less noble response. God then warned Cain about his wrong attitude and its potential consequences, saying, "Sin is crouching at your door; it desires to have you, but you must master it" (verse 7).

Two men, two choices, two paths. What choice did man #1 make? Cain chose to allow sin to master him and failed the test for handling temptation God's way. His jealousy toward his brother Abel and God's acceptance of Abel's gift caused him to sink deeper into sin and ultimately to murder his brother. In the end, Cain's inability to handle temptation disqualified him from God's blessing and from any influence for good with his life. His choice led him down a path of destruction.

Jesus—Man #2 lived thousands of years after the days of Cain and Abel. This man, too, faced temptation. This man was Jesus. After 40 days of fasting in a physically weakened state, Jesus was tempted by Satan in three different areas of life. With all three temptations, Jesus fought back, quoting the Word of God (Luke 4:1-12). Jesus chose to withstand the temptations. He passed the tests perfectly and thus walked the path of positive influence, impacting the entire world—the path that led to the cross, the path that led to your salvation and mine. The tale of these two men looks like this:

Two Men:	Cain	Jesus
Two choices:	gave in	withstood
Two paths:	murdered brother	saved many
Two results:	destruction	influence

Your Choice, Your Path

The choices of these two men give you and me some very sobering lessons on the importance of dealing with temptation and sin. Did you notice that I wrote both *temptation* and *sin*? That's because they're different. Temptation is not sin. Cain was tempted—sin was "crouching at the door." He *could* have chosen to resist the temptation and therefore not to sin, but *didn't*. Jesus was tempted, but He *did* resist the temptations.

How about you? How are you dealing with your past, your thoughts, your temptations? Where are your choices leading you? What direction is your path taking you? I'm sure that you, like me, are not always pleased with the way you handle (or fail to handle!) temptation.

Take heart, my fellow-struggler. God has provided a way for us to stand up under the struggle against temptation and choose to move down the path of influence. As 1 Corinthians 10:13 says, "God is faithful; he will not let you be tempted beyond what you can bear. But when you are tempted, he will also provide a way out so that you can stand up under it."

God's Provision for Our Temptations

First, God has provided a new law—A law is a fixed way in which things work. For instance, the law of gravity says that anything heavier than air will fall. That means that if you jump off a ten-story building, you will fall to your death. But there are laws that counter the law of gravity—the laws of aerodynamics. These laws allow a 747 jumbo jet, filled with hundreds of people and weighing hundreds of thousands of pounds, to fly.

In like manner, when you and I come to Christ, God counters the law of sin and death—a law that gave us no choice, only death. But when we come to a saving knowledge of Jesus Christ, we come under the influence of a new law—the law of the Spirit of life in Christ (Romans 8:2). This new law sets us free from the bondage of sin. Through this new law, we now have the power to choose to resist temptation.

Second, God has provided a guide—A guide is someone or something that leads you through unfamiliar territory and keeps you from getting lost. Jesus promised He would give believers a "guide" to live in them and always be with them. That guide is the Holy Spirit, who lives in all believers and guides them into all truth (John 16:13). When you and I came to Christ, this promise from Jesus became true for us. As a result, we now have our own guide—the Holy Spirit—who leads us throughout all of life and through all the situations we will ever face in life.

Third, God has provided a guidebook—God has also given us our own personal guidebook, the Bible. Everything we need to know about life and godly living is presented to us in God's Word, the Bible (2 Peter 1:3). This guidebook gives us the answers for dealing with every kind of temptation.

Fourth, God has provided guides—God has also provided us with other believers who can encourage us to resist and overcome the temptations of this world. That's why it is so important for you to be involved in a local church. There you can find other more mature men who can hold you accountable and guide you with wise counsel. I am personally thankful to God for the many men of influence who have served as faithful, caring guides to me. These "soldiers of the cross" have been and are committed to watching over my spiritual growth on the battlefield of life.

Now, you may be thinking in your mind, *But Jim doesn't know my situation. He can't know the pressures I'm under—pressures on my job, in my marriage, with my children, from the baggage of my past life of sin. I can't help but succumb to temptation. No matter how hard I try, I can't seem to overcome certain sins!*

Well, you're right. I don't know what specific issues you are struggling with. But I do know that you are not alone. Temptation is universal. The Bible says it is "*common* to man" (1 Corinthians 10:13). That means you and I and all other men struggle with the same temptations and sins. That's the bad news.

But the good news is that God has provided a way out, an escape and victory (1 Corinthians 10:13 and 15:57). With these four resources—

a new law (life in Christ),

a guide (the Holy Spirit),

a guidebook (the Bible), and

guides (wise counselors)—

we have the ability to withstand the temptations that confront us in our daily living. Statements of "I can't" no longer apply to us. Now, in Jesus Christ, it's "I can!" Paul tells us to "be strong in the Lord, and in his mighty power" (Ephesians 6:10).

So the next time you are confronted with an opportunity to sin (like in the next millisecond!) remember, "I *can* do everything through him who gives me strength" (Philippians 4:13). God has given you the *I can* to deal with that temptation. But you must supply the *I will*. It's your choice. Your path and your influence is at stake! No choice is a small choice. And no choice is a meaningless choice.

The Devil Made Me Do It

Before we move to our next chapter, there's one more issue we need to address.

Have you ever heard the statement, "The devil made me do it"? For most of us the devil is a convenient "fall guy." We blame him for our bad conduct, our wrong actions, and our failures. Everything is the devil's fault, not ours. Therefore you and I don't have to be responsible. Why should we, if we think the devil is responsible for our wrong behavior? It's like the lady who told the famous preacher, Donald Grey Barnhouse, after he informed his congregation they could no longer blame Satan for all their problems: "Dr. Barnhouse, I was disappointed in the message. You said we can't blame Satan. But Satan has always been such a comfort to me."

No, the devil doesn't make us sin. He doesn't need to! Oh, he may assist us or even facilitate our sin. But in most cases he merely provides the opportunities with his worldly schemes... and we, who so often find it hard to say no to sin and our flesh, willingly do the rest.

Suffice it to say, you and I should never again think, "The devil made me do it." It just isn't true!

So what can we do? How can we handle temptation? Don't fail to read the next chapter and its lifesaving message about how to handle three different types of temptation.

Fortune. Fame. Power. Pleasure.
When it comes to temptation, these are the biggies.
These…represent the weakest links in our chain of
resistance…the most obvious chinks in our armor.
If the enemy of our souls wants to launch
one of his "flaming missiles"
toward an area that will have the greatest impact,
he's got a choice of…targets.
—CHARLES R. SWINDOLL[30]

Fighting the Battle Against Temptation

Put on the full armor of God
so that you can take your stand....
—Ephesians 6:11

"War is hell!"

That's the quote I often heard from my Dad, who was a soldier who fought in Germany during World War II. But a generation later, as I sat in a classroom at Fort Bragg, North Carolina, I was hearing it again...and beginning to feel the full force of the words, "War is hell!"

How did I come to be sitting in a war classroom at Fort Bragg? My U.S. Army Reserve medical unit was called up for active duty during the Bosnian crisis in the 1990s. We were on our way to Germany to take over the duties of a regular Army hospital corps that had been deployed to the battlefront in Bosnia. So there I sat, receiving a combat briefing. I was listening to instructors lecture on land mines, snipers, mortar attacks, chemical warfare, and so on. It was clear that the Army wanted our group to be prepared for any and every danger we might face in battle.

Life Is a Battle

Living the Christian life is a battle, too. (And if you don't think so, then you just might not be living the Christian life very successfully!) Jesus Himself told us, "In this world you will have trouble" (John 16:33). That trouble for us men comes in a variety of packages. And, like my Army instructors, God wants us to prepare for the inevitable battle. Therefore, for us to be properly prepared, we must know what God's Word, the Bible, says about the temptations we will face as we go through life.

Most of us don't need a list of the temptations we struggle with every day. But, just in case you or I have forgotten what they are, the Bible gives us a list. Galatians 5:19 says, "The acts of the sinful nature are obvious"—and then the list reads:

> sexual immorality, impurity and debauchery; idolatry and witchcraft; hatred, discord, jealousy, fits of rage, selfish ambition, dissensions, factions and envy; drunkenness, orgies, and the like (Galatians 5:19-21).

Pretty awful, isn't it? So how can we get a handle on these temptations and fight the battle against them? I am most grateful to Dr. Curtis Mitchell, now retired from Biola University, La Mirada, California, grouping temptations into three types.

Type A: Temptations of the Flesh

We as men are bombarded with *all* of the temptations in God's list in Galatians 5:19-21 *all* of the time. But I'm sure you agree that sensual and sexual temptation—Type-A temptation—is a frequent and critical problem for Christian men today and a universal problem for every man. You and I can hardly take a step or live a minute without being assaulted with a Type-A temptation, which is mainly triggered through the "eye gate." That makes the children's song lyric—"be careful, little eyes, what you see"—especially applicable for this type of sin, a line that would have helped the Old Testament king, David!

David's sin with the woman Bathsheba is a perfect example of a man who struggled with a Type-A temptation (see 2 Samuel 11:1-5). What happened? The Bible explains it this way: David "*saw* a woman bathing. The woman was very beautiful [How did he know this, other than by a lingering look?] and David *sent* someone to find out about her" (verses 2-3)...and, well, you know the rest of the story. "David sent messengers to *get* her...and he *slept* with her" (verse 4).

But here's what I want you to notice: David's sin started with the eyes (which is true for many of the Type-A temptations). David could have stopped the process at any time, but he chose (there's that word again) to proceed and to sin sexually with Bathsheba. He made the wrong choices. In fact, he made a *string* of wrong choices!

Now, the issue is, how can you and I protect ourselves against Type-A temptations, and especially those of a sensual nature?

First and foremost, always remember that God has provided "a way of escape" (1 Corinthians 10:13 NASB). Then follow these practical suggestions for defending yourself.

- *Pursue godliness*—The best defense is a good offense. Therefore pursue a life of godliness (2 Timothy 2:22). How? By reading God's Word, by worshiping with God's people, and by being accountable to one or more of God's men. Don't be a defenseless, defeated warrior. Don't give in to the temptation. Fight the battle for your purity with all the resources that God has provided.

- *Avoid places and situations where you might be tempted*—Stay away from old haunts, magazine racks with sensual covers on display, and being alone with a woman other than your wife (does this sound familiar?). "*Flee* the evil desires of youth" was

Paul's advice to his young disciple (2 Timothy 2:22). And brother, it's good advice for you and me as well!

- *Avoid people who might tempt you*—I spoke earlier of "friends" who pull you down. So I'll say it again. Be careful about buddies from the past and friends from the present who have a lower standard than you want for your life. Avoid anyone who might drag you down. Follow this wise advice from the book of Proverbs (known as "the book of wisdom") and keep your path far from them. "If sinners entice you, do not give in to them....do not go along with them, do not set foot on their paths" (Proverbs 1:10,15).

- *Avoid allowing your eyes to roam*—I used to have a sales manager who, as I would describe it, could undress a woman with his eyes. Don't be that kind of man. Determine to do what Job did when he "made a covenant with [his] eyes not to look lustfully at a girl" (Job 31:1).

Type-A temptations arise from the desires of our flesh. You and I don't need a lot of help from the devil with this type of temptation! No, our own sinful flesh spurs us along.

Type B: Temptations of the World

Whereas Type-A temptations are usually sensual and of the *flesh*, Type-B temptations go deeper into the *heart*. If Type-A temptations involve *girls*, Type-B temptations involve *gold* and *glory*, the temptations that relate to life and living. This type of appeal is called "the boasting of what [a man] has and does" and "the boastful pride of life" (1 John 2:16 NASB).

So often you and I are tempted with desires for money, possessions, and pleasures. These Type-B temptations rob us of a heart and a passion for God and the things of God. Here's how they work…

In terms of generational categories, I am what's frequently described as a "baby boomer." My parents came out of World War II with nothing but dreams of a better life for themselves and for me. I grew up with a focus on "the good life." That obsession, if you please, led me away from the Lord. Years later I recognized the emptiness of such a lifestyle. Then, like the prodigal son in the Bible, I realized how far away I was from God and returned home to a forgiving heavenly Father (Luke 15:11-32).

What a trap our materialistic society can lay for us! Now, don't get me wrong. You may be a man who successfully handles these kinds of worldly temptations. But I didn't. And we can all fall, so…just be careful!

Now meet Lot. His story gives you and me an archetype of a Type-B temptation. You'll want to read Genesis 13:1-13 for the whole story. But in a nutshell, Lot, who was Abraham's nephew, was given a choice of where to live and raise his herds. The Bible says Lot "looked up and *saw* that the whole plain of the Jordan was well watered.…So Lot *chose* for himself the whole plain of the Jordan" (verses 10-11).

Do you want to hear God's comment on Lot's choice? He records, "Now the men of Sodom were *wicked* and were *sinning* greatly against the LORD" (verse 13). (Have you ever heard of Sodom and Gomorrah?!) While Lot's choice may have seemed to be the right *practical* business decision, it led to *spiritual* disaster for him and his family (see Genesis 19).

So what's to keep you from falling into the same trap that Lot (and I) fell into—Type-B temptations—temptations of worldliness and materialism?

- *Develop a love for God*—that withstands the pull of the world. Love grows with familiarity, so become familiar with God through reading His Word.

"The love of wealth makes bitter men; the love of God, better men."[31]

- *Understand the lie*—that the pleasures of this world are worth giving up what really matters... like your relationship with God, your family, your reputation, and your influence. Understand that the world is ebbing away...but doing the will of God has eternal rewards (1 John 2:17).

- *Realize the spiritual implications*—that every decision, including business decisions, can have. Remember Lot!

- *Guard against*—an unhealthy focus on the "good life." Theologically, wealth has the potential to create more serious problems than poverty does.

- *Remember*—that you cannot serve the world and serve God at the same time (Matthew 6:24). A man of influence seeks the kingdom of God first (verse 33).

- *Realize*—that the more encumbered you are with the world, the less freedom you have to serve God. As missionary Albert Sweitzer discovered, "Anything you own that you cannot give away, you don't own it, it owns you."

- *Pray daily*—that God would give you the wisdom and strength you need to fight against worldliness. "It is the daily drill which makes the battle hero."[32]

Type C: Temptations of the Devil

Do you remember my comment earlier that the devil is blamed for a lot of our temptations? As well as my statement that we are quite capable of sinning on our own, especially when it comes to Type-A and Type-B temptations? Well, Type-C temptations are more directly involved with the devil. These are the temptations of the *soul*. These are temptations which frequently deal with the nature and character of God. These are temptations to think ignoble thoughts of God. Let me illustrate...

Eve, the mother of all, was created and placed in the Garden of Eden to be Adam's helper and life partner (Genesis 2:18-22). Then, some time later, when Eve was alone, she was approached by "the serpent," who proceeded to tempt Eve to doubt God's character. Satan queried, "Did God *really* say...?" (Genesis 3:1). Satan worked Eve over by planting seeds of doubt regarding God's character and God's instructions until she gave in, disobeyed God, and ate of the forbidden fruit.

Brother, ever since that day, Satan has continued to ply his schemes to get us to mistrust God. So how do we deal with these kinds of temptations?

- *Gain a better understanding of God's attributes and God's character*—We learn what God is like by reading His Word. And when we don't read His Word, we tend to forget what He is like and fail to trust Him. And Satan loves a man with "spiritual amnesia"!

- *Gain a better understanding of Satan's tactics*—Satan loves to confuse people when it comes to theology (the study of God). If he can get you and me to have a distorted view of God, then, chances are, he can get us to have a distorted view of life, our conduct, and our accountability to a holy God. Instead, you and I must "be strong in the Lord and in his mighty power. Put on the full armor of God so that you can take your stand against the devil's schemes" (Ephesians 6:12).

- *Gain a better understanding of God's Word*—Build an arsenal of Scripture verses to use whenever you are tempted. Jesus fought the devil with the Word of God, constantly saying, "It is written….It is written….It is written" (Matthew 4:4-7). Are you well armed? Do you know *what* is written? Are you fighting your battles against temptation with the sword of the Spirit, which is the Word of God (Ephesians 6:17)?

Seeking God's Help in the Battle

Brother, let's agree to fight the battle against temptation with our eyes wide open! Here are the cold, hard facts: Temptation is ongoing. As long as you and I are alive and breathing, we will be dealing with every sin and temptation on every level—Type A, Type B, and Type C. The battle is raging in every area of your life, and will ultimately be fought at every stage of your life. Whether you are a young man struggling with the temptations of the flesh, a middle-aged man tempted with worldliness and desires for fame, fortune, and "the good life," or a man in his sunset years who begins to doubt the sufficiency of God's promises and provision as you contemplate death, you (and every man) can be certain the temptations will never go away.

The question is, will you allow God to fight your battle for you through the resources He has given you? Or will you try to go it alone? Your future is riding on how you deal with temptation. *How you and I handle our temptations will drastically mark the level of our ability to influence others for God.*

Why is the quality of your secret life vital?
Because it's your inner life. And brother,
the inner life is where life's battles
are fought…and won.
It encompasses your mind…
what you think and think on.
It includes your will…what you decide
you will and won't do.
And it centers on your heart.
—Jim George

Looking at Your Secret Life

Therefore we do not lose heart.
Though outwardly we are wasting away,
yet inwardly we are being renewed day by day.
—2 Corinthians 4:16

Several years ago my wife and I were in Alaska for a joint speaking engagement. On Saturday afternoon, while the ladies were finishing up their part of the conference, a commercial fisherman treated me to a trip around Petersburg Bay on his fishing boat. What a thrill! We saw sea lions, seals, eagles, and even several whales. But what inspired the greatest awe (and fear!) in me was the icebergs. The captain of the boat, exercising great caution, steered clear of them. Clearly he, too, was in awe of them!

In fact, the captain made a very wide berth around one particularly large berg. As we circled the frozen mass he explained why icebergs are so feared and respected. Seven-eights of the mass of an iceberg is below the surface. We were only seeing one-eighth of the total mass. How far out did the ice really extend under the water? The captain couldn't know. All we could do was view its ominous presence with great respect... and from a great distance!

Friend, what's true about icebergs is true about our lives. That's the way our life should be. Our secret life, our inner life, our private life is much like the mass of an iceberg, which is below the surface, away from the public eye. Just as an iceberg's strength and power comes largely from the unseen portion, it's the secret part of our life that's unseen by others that gives us our power to have an outward and awesome influence.

Recognizing the Importance of Your Secret Life

I don't know if you've noticed this, but in the previous 13 chapters, we've been looking long and hard at the secret life of a man of influence has to do with our secret life. I call it "the secret life" because it's the private life of a man, the part of us no one sees. The "inner man" is what the Bible calls it. As we've talked about obedience, setting goals, spiritual discipline, and temptation, we've been learning about changing who we are on the inside—your secret life.

And why is the quality of your secret life vital? Because that is where life's battles are fought...and won. The inner life encompasses your mind...what you think and think on. It includes your will...what you decide you will and won't do. And it centers on your heart. As the Bible says, "as [a man] thinketh in his heart, so is he" (Proverbs 23:7 KJV).

Well, my friend, it is as a man *desires* to become a man of influence that he begins to win the battle of the secret life. You and I must want that vibrant inner life badly enough to pay the price of growth and spiritual maturity. But what a blessed reward will be ours if we are willing to pay the price—we will become men of influence!

Nurturing Your Secret Life

In my book *A Man After God's Own Heart*, I share a little of my struggle with my Christian walk and how one day I woke up to the reality of my disobedience. That was the beginning of my desire to "return home" in my walk with the Lord. From that point on I have diligently, carefully, seriously, and painstakingly been nurturing my secret life. It's not always been easy. In fact, I've faced many struggles. But by God's grace, it's been a joyous and exciting journey of growth and some measure of influence.

But enough about me. Now for you. What will godly desire and a carefully nurtured secret life produce in your life? What kind of man will you become as you follow through on your desire to become a man of influence, a man who makes a lasting impact? According to the "secrets" revealed in the last 13 chapters, the process will look something like this...

- You are developing deep personal convictions. These convictions will come from your desire to be obedient in all areas of your life to your Lord Jesus Christ.

- You are subordinating all of your life under a set of God-centered goals—goals that embrace all of the major areas of a man's life.

- You are establishing and maintaining a personal life of discipline—understanding that spiritual discipline and physical discipline are bound as one.

- You are making wiser and more biblical decisions. Why? Because you are beginning to understand that the essence of the Christian life resides in the will.

- You are embracing the concept of influence—your godly influence on others.

- You are accepting the challenge of living a godly life—a life that will have an influence on others.

- You are understanding that to have an influence on people you must establish the right priorities in your life...and people must be one of your top priorities.

- You are sensing that your life has purpose and destiny. Why? Because you are beginning to perceive yourself as a man of God whose life is significant, as one who wants to leave behind a lasting impact.

What a powerful force you and I can be in the hands of God! But it starts with our secret life. So what's it to be? Develop the secret life and expand your influence...or foolishly squander away the gift of a life meant to influence others and leave an indelible mark? I think I know your answer. You wouldn't have read this far if you, like me, didn't have a desire to have a greater impact. So I trust what you've read about the secrets of a life of influence has encouraged you regarding the importance of cultivating your inner life. For as I've just said, a life of great public influence starts by nurturing a deep, private inner life.

Illustrating the Influence of Your Secret Life

That boat trip in Alaska made for a memorable day! The experience was unforgettable. And my encounter with that large iceberg left me impressed and awed. And, my dear friend, that's the way it can be with your life and mine...if we settle once and for all the issue of the necessity of nurturing our secret life according to God's Word. Then the results of our inner change will emerge above the surface to leave a breathtaking and lasting impact on others.

While I was writing about the huge iceberg in Alaska, I thought of another illustration that pictures well how our secret life affects our outer life. Some of the mightiest mountains are created when hot molten lava is pushed from the depths beneath the earth and shoots upward above the surface. As I see it, the force of the underground pressure of our secret life pushes our inner character upward and onward until we stand tall as a mountain, jutting forth for all to behold.

Isn't that a great way to picture your life? As an awesome iceberg? As a majestic mountain? All because you've nurtured the inner man according to God's ways.

So, friend, what are the outward signs that indicate you and I have faithfully nurtured our inner life? What are the visible marks of a life of influence? In our remaining chapters we will look at the external evidences of internal vitality. These signs are the "payoff" for the time and care we take with our underground life with God, the payoff for nurturing heart and soul. These evidences are what make us into men of influence.

Influence is based on character.
And character is developed in secret.

Part 2:

The Signs of a Life of Influence

Tied to
the value of the person
is the principle of servanthood.
We value what we freely serve.
—Douglas Groothuis [33]

A HEART FOR SERVING

Surely you remember, brothers,
our toil and hardship; we worked night and day
in order not to be a burden to anyone
while we preached the gospel of God to you.
—1 THESSALONIANS 2:9

One nice feature of Southern California is the weather. Normally the climate is mild, even during the winter months. But on one particular day in mid-January, the weather was unusually cold and rainy. But more than the abnormal weather condition, what made this an especially memorable day was the sad scene I witnessed at a cemetery. I was there because, several days earlier, a local funeral home called and asked me to officiate at a graveside service for a man who didn't have a pastor or a church in the area. I was eager to participate because I saw this as an opportunity to help out the man's family and to share the good news of Jesus Christ with those who attended.

When the day arrived, I made sure I got to the cemetery early so I could meet the man's family and friends and give them some words of encouragement in the midst of his death. The funeral director met me and the two of us began our graveside vigil. Finally, well past the time for the service to begin, a lone car came through the gate of the cemetery and stopped on the road that led to the casket, which rested under a canopy. In the car was the wife of the deceased.

Hurrying out of the car, the out-of-breath woman asked how long the service would last. She announced that she didn't have much time, and besides, she explained, her late husband hadn't had much time for anyone either. And now, as was obvious, no one had time for him or his service. I conducted the service in the driving rain with only the funeral director and the impatient wife present.

What a Difference a Life Makes!

Now contrast the above scene with another funeral I participated in. Stan Miller had served as a pastor and hospital chaplain for more than 40 years. Stan was a man with a heart for serving. At his memorial service dozens of people, including his wife, children, and grand- and great-grandchildren, stood up and gave testimony to the impact Stan had on their lives. He had sacrificially loved his wife for more than 50 years. He had sacrificed for the education of his children. And he had continually sacrificed his time, money, and energies for others. The room was filled with hundreds of others, including myself, who had been impacted by Stan's life of service.

Like I said, this was quite a contrast to the other funeral!

—The first man was a taker his whole life and left nothing behind. As I drove away from his grave site, I looked into my rearview mirror and, from all appearances, there was little visible proof that this man ever existed.

—The other man was a giver his whole life and left a legacy of influence behind. Hundreds were living proof of the lasting impact of his life of service.

That's the next principle we're going to look at. A man of influence has a heart for serving others.

Two Examples of a Servant

A heart for serving others is one of the qualities developed in our secret life. Yet it can be easily seen by others. In the short time my wife and I have been members of our present church, we have witnessed this heart for service in the lives of the church leaders. And I also have to say that over the years, I have been fortunate to see this mark of influence demonstrated by numerous other men. Now let's look at two incidents involving two men of influence who give us what I believe to be the best demonstrations of what it means to have a heart for serving.

Jesus Christ—I'm sure you agree that Jesus Christ was the most influential man who has ever lived. No one has ever or will ever have the impact on history that this one man has had. Why? There's one very important reason—Jesus Christ was deity in human flesh. But, as you read your New Testament, you don't see God-the-Son as an autocrat, a leader running roughshod over people or demanding respect and obedience. No, you see just the opposite! You see a humble servant.

Now, try to place yourself in this scene. In John chapter 13, we see God, in human flesh, taking a towel and a basin of water and kneeling down before His creation, His followers, and His subordinates, and washing their dirty feet. This has to be one of the greatest examples of servanthood ever recorded in history!

Sometime when you're having your devotions, read John 13:1-17 for yourself to get the full effect of this example of a servant's heart in action. Jesus' message to His disciples—and to us!—is this: "I have set you an example that you should do as I have done for you" (John 13:15). How could we not obey? So I ask you, Whose feet could you wash today? Who in your family needs you to come alongside as a servant? Who at church craves the helping hand of your service?

Dwight L. Moody—A second man who demonstrated the heart of a servant is the famous nineteenth-century Chicago preacher, D.L. Moody.

One year in the late 1800s, a large group of European pastors came to Moody's Northfield Bible Conference. The European pastors, following their custom of the time, put their shoes outside their rooms the first night to be cleaned by the "hall servant." But, the conference being in America, there were no hall servants.

That night, as Moody walked the halls of the dormitory praying for the conference and those in attendance, he saw the shoes. Not wanting to embarrass his visitors, Moody mentioned the need to some young ministerial students...who piously excused themselves from helping. So the world's most famous evangelist of his day returned to the dorm, gathered up the dirty shoes, took them to his room, and cleaned and polished every shoe himself. The deed would have gone unnoticed except for the entrance of a friend who witnessed the event.

The next morning, the European pastors opened their doors to find shiny, spotless shoes. Moody told no one what he had done. But his friend told a few people, and then an amazing thing happened. During the remainder of the conference, different men secretly volunteered each night to shine the shoes of their guests.

Both Jesus Christ and D.L. Moody are prime examples of men who had a heart for serving. Both were men of true greatness and influence. Both demonstrate for us the impact a man can have when he develops a heart for serving others.

Insights on Becoming a Servant

I hope you're catching the spirit of what it means to be a man of influence. And I hope you now see how being a servant is key to having an impact. As I said at the outset of our profiling journey, the apostle Paul is always an excellent person to examine and re-examine as a man of profound influence. The impact of his life is still being felt today. Why? Because he, like his Master, Jesus, and like the great D.L. Moody, was a man with a heart for serving others.

So consider these insights on becoming a servant from the heart and life of Paul. Let's join up with him in Acts 17:2. Here, we learn that Paul spent "three Sabbath days" reasoning from the Scriptures with the Jews in the local synagogue in Thessalonica, a town in Macedonia (now modern Greece). We don't know exactly how much longer Paul was there because (as usual!) the Jews became jealous, started a riot, and forced Paul to leave town. Listen now as Paul reflects on his time with the Thessalonians. And pay close attention as he gives us nine insights on being a servant, as stated in 1 Thessalonians 2:1-12.

Insight #1: *Serve for a higher purpose*—Sometimes we do an act of service and then get the feeling that our service didn't count...that nobody noticed or cares...that it really didn't matter...that the whole thing was a failure. Or at other times we serve and our service seems to go unnoticed. But that's okay! Paul had all the same feelings, yet he wrote, "You know, brothers, that our visit to you was not a failure" (1 Thessalonians 2:1). In other words, service for a higher purpose—for God's purposes—is never a failure, no matter what!

Do you remember the man Mordecai in the Old Testament book of Esther? Mordecai was the cousin of Queen Esther. And one day, while Mordecai was sitting in the gate (a place of influence in those days), he overheard a plot to kill the king. He then informed Esther...who informed her husband, the king, giving the credit to Mordecai...and the plot was foiled. How much time passed before Mordecai was recognized for his service to the king? Five long years later, the king realized that Mordecai had not been properly rewarded! Could you wait five years to be thanked for your service? Would you continue to serve even if it seemed your service went unnoticed or appeared to be a failure?

But here's Paul's message to us. If you and I serve for a higher purpose, God's purpose, then results or thank yous or recognition and rewards don't matter. Why? Because our service was done unto God. And that's our higher purpose—to please God. That's all that matters. John Whiteley, a nine-teenth-century missionary to New Zealand, got it right when he penned these words:

> I thank God that I can say my duty is my delight, and the encouraging proofs I have that I do not labor in vain or spend my strength for nought encourages me to "Labour on at God's command, and offer all my work to Him."[34]

Insight #2: *Serve in spite of your situation*—In other words, if you or I wait until conditions are perfect, we will never serve. Paul was a man who served in spite of his situation. He reported that "we dared to tell you his gospel *in spite of* strong opposition" (1 Thessalonians 2:2)—the opposition of the religious leaders, of rioters, and of imprisonment.

Another one of God's servants, Moses, had to choose to serve in spite of his situation, too. Moses was called by God to lead His people out of Egypt (Exodus 3:1-22). But there was just one problem—the people weren't sure they wanted Moses to lead them anywhere! Moses' situation was bleak.

- Moses had no credibility as a leader—he had only led sheep for 40 years.

- Moses had no authority—he came as an outsider.

- Moses had no human resources—he had only a staff.

- Moses had no help—he was later given his brother, Aaron, as an assistant.

How would you respond to this kind of commission and in this kind of situation? You and I would probably respond as Moses did, offering up a multitude of excuses about why we couldn't possibly serve. Well, Moses finally accepted God's call to service. And he went on to lead God's people out of Egypt. Then he faithfully served God for 40 more years while the Israelites wandered in the wilderness. In the end, God called Moses "my *servant* Moses" (Numbers 12:7). Moses' circumstances weren't easy, but he passed the test. Like Paul, Moses served in spite of his situation.

Now let's fast-forward more than 3,000 years to today...and to you. What is God asking you to do for Him in the way of service? Are you giving Him excuses as to why you cannot serve in your situation? Contemplate this advice from T.J. Bach, missionary to Venezuela: "If we are going to wait until every possible hindrance has been removed before we do a work for the Lord, we will never attempt to do anything."[35]

Like Paul, who served in the midst of opposition and persecution, and like Moses, who served under extreme difficulty, and like Mr. Bach, God's missionary to a foreign land, you too ought to be willing to serve your Lord, no matter what the situation. So, fill in the blank:

Yes, Lord, I am willing to serve You in spite of

_____.

There's more to learn about developing a heart for serving, and in the next chapter, we'll get to the remaining seven insights on service. But for now, think about this simple-yet-profound principle of influence...

If you want to influence others,
you must start by serving others.

When you think of servanthood,
do you envision it as an activity
performed by relatively low-skilled people
at the bottom of the positional totem pole?
If you do, you have a wrong impression.
Servanthood is not about position or skill.
It's about attitude.[36]
—JOHN MAXWELL

An Attitude of Servanthood

Whoever wants to become great among you
must be your servant...
just as the Son of Man
did not come to be served, but to serve....
—MATTHEW 20:26, 28

I've always considered myself to be a man's man. I loved and participated in sports during my high school years. I also watch my share of sporting events (and faithfully follow the Oklahoma Sooners!). So please don't think of me as strange when I say I also have an interest in poetry. Have you seen the television commercial with the wrestler Hulk Hogan reciting his poetry? Well, I'm no Hulk Hogan, but I have written a volume of rhymes for boys drawn from the book of Proverbs.[37] And here is my attempt to paraphrase the scripture above from Matthew 20:

> Do you want to be great?
> Do you want to be grand?
> Do you want to have influence
> on those at hand?
>
> Then learn to be a servant
> who's humble and true,
> Doing God's will
> your whole life through.

Ah, hmmm…let's quickly move on!

Jesus' disciples had the common-but-mistaken notion that lordship equaled leadership. Being the great leaders they thought they were, James and John, two of Jesus' disciples, asked their mother(!) to petition Jesus for two seats of prominence in Jesus' future kingdom. They thought that if they could sit in seats of influence (that is, at His right and His left), they would then be great men of influence (Matthew 20:20-21). But Jesus said just the opposite is true. He said, in essence, "If you want to have influence at the highest level, be willing to serve at the lowest level" (see Matthew 20:25-28).

As Jesus pointed out, greatness (influence) comes from being willing to serve. And in 1 Thessalonians 2:1-12, Paul gives nine insights about servanthood. So far we've learned that #1) we are to serve with a higher purpose, and #2) we are to serve in spite of our situation. Let's look now at more of Paul's insights.

Insights on Becoming a Servant

Insight #3: *Serve with integrity*—Have you ever thought about the fact that what you believe actually determines how you behave? Your integrity comes from a correct belief system. The integrity of our service, then, is built on a right understanding of God and His Word. That's why Paul could say to those whom he served in Thessalonica, "The appeal we make does not spring from error or impure motives" (1 Thessalonians 2:3).

The title "public servant" is often used to speak of our government officials. The men and women in public office have been elected by "we the people" and are in office to serve us. At the beginning of our country's history, public service and integrity were seen as indivisible. But sad to say, in today's society, integrity and service are no longer seen as dual requirements for government officials. You can serve in government without integrity.

But that's not God's standard for service. Integrity is an indispensable quality for God's servants to possess. For example, consider the character of the men who were carefully and prayerfully selected as servers in the church in Acts 6:3. They were to be "men of good reputation, full of the Spirit and of wisdom" (NASB). And what was the important task they were asked to do? To serve tables! Friend, we are to serve with integrity no matter what God asks us to do—even if it's serving tables—because we serve a holy God who demands integrity from us, His servants.

Insight #4: *Serve to please God*—Every time you and I serve, we must ask, Who am I serving? If our service is done to please men, then we will not be servants of God. We can't do both. Paul knew that. So he declared up front, "we speak as men approved by God...not trying to please men" (1 Thessalonians 2:4). Listen as Paul explains elsewhere:

> Am I now trying to win the approval of
> men, or of God? Or am I trying to please men?
> If I were still trying to please men, I would not
> be a servant of Christ (Galatians 1:10).

Aaron, the brother of Moses, was of great help during the exodus of the children of Israel and in the beginning of the trip to the Promised Land. But Aaron had a problem—he was a man-pleaser. While Moses was on Mount Sinai for 40 days receiving the Ten Commandments from God, the people became restless. They began to wonder if Moses was still alive. They asked Aaron to "make us gods who will go before us" (Exodus 32:1). Aaron immediately caved in to their request and made them a golden calf to worship (verses 2-6).

You see, Aaron had a choice. He could have resisted the demands of the people and said, "No way!" and thus he would have been serving God. Instead, he served the people and not

God. Now do you see why it's vital for us to ask, Who am I serving?

Insight #5: *Serve with pure motives*—Whereas the previous insight dealt with pleasing men, this insight deals with pleasing ourselves. Okay, so you're not a man-pleaser. That's good! But...do you love the praise others give when you serve? Do you outwardly refuse the thanks and attention others give you while inwardly you are saying, "Keep the praise coming...give me more!"? Not so with Paul! He served with pure motives from the start: "We never used flattery, nor did we put on a mask to cover up greed....We were not looking for praise" (1 Thessalonians 2:5-6).

The Bible tells it like it is—"the heart is deceitful above all things" (Jeremiah 17:9). And Jeremiah, the writer of this truth, adds that the heart is "beyond cure"! Is your service done for the praise you receive from others? Check your heart, and make sure your motives are pure.

Insight #6: *Serve with love*—There is no greater example of loving service than that seen in a mother. Those of us who are married and have children have seen the loving service our wives give to our children when they are sick, when they suffer in any way or at any time. I'm sure that's why our little ones love to snuggle up against their mother. The servant attitude of love is what you and I must offer in our service as well.

And that's the attitude with which Paul served others. He put it this way: "We were gentle among you, like a mother.... We loved you...we were delighted to share...our lives as well... because you had become so dear to us" (1 Thessalonians 2:7-8). Love is a fruit of the Spirit (Galatians 5:22), and it is Spirit-empowered love that will energize your service anywhere it is needed. (And, don't forget that attitude of love starts right in your own home with your self-sacrificing love for your wife and your beautiful children!)

Insight #7: *Serve sacrificially*—By definition, a servant sacrifices for the needs of the ones he serves. The question is, how much are you willing to give in your service for the needs of others? Paul said he was willing to work night and day to serve. He wrote, "Surely you remember, brothers, our toil and hardship; we worked night and day in order not to be a burden to anyone" (verse 9). Do you have that kind of attitude when you are asked to serve? Do you serve sacrificially?

As I write this, I thought of another man who served others sacrificially. We don't even know his name, but we do know of his sacrificial deeds. His story is told by Jesus in Luke 10:30-37. We call him the Good Samaritan. Let me list his sacrificial service on behalf of a complete stranger:

- He sacrificed time by stopping to help a wounded man.

- He sacrificed his possessions by bandaging and dressing the man's wounds.

- He sacrificed his personal transportation by carrying the man to an inn.

- He sacrificed his life by personally taking care of the man.

- He sacrificed his money by giving a day's wages and a blank check to an innkeeper as an advance payment for the continued care of the wounded man.

This, brother, is what it means to serve sacrificially. Do you think the Samaritan had an influence on the wounded man? The Bible doesn't say, but we can only imagine the impact!

As you read through the story of the Good Samaritan, you will also notice two other men mentioned—a priest and a Levite. They, too, saw the wounded man...and walked by on the other side of the road. They had no contact with the man in need. Therefore they had no impact, and obviously, no influence. I think you will agree with me, as this story so graphically illustrates, that *the greater the sacrifice one makes, the greater the influence one can make.*

Insight #8: *Serve blamelessly*—This insight into the heart of Paul takes us back to Insight #3, *Serve with integrity.* Paul wrote, "You are witnesses, and so is God, of how holy, righteous and blameless we were among you" (1 Thessalonians 2:10). The word "blameless" means that no one can bring a charge against you. You are a "Teflon Christian"—no accusation can stick against you. Again, do you think God wants His servants to be pure? I think you know the answer—*yes!* That's why God requires that His servant-leaders be "above reproach" (1 Timothy 3:2) and "blameless" (Titus 1:6). And dear brother, God requires this same standard for you and me as well. When you and I strive to have a life that is pure, our service will take on a blameless quality. Our service will be motivated by the desire to please God and selflessly assist others.

Insight #9: *Serve to nurture*—Do you realize that even if you say nothing to those you serve, you are still teaching volumes? You nurture others by your Christlike example of selfless service. Paul did this. He explains, "We dealt with each of you as a father deals with his own children, encouraging, comforting and urging you to live lives worthy of God" (1 Thessalonians 2:11-12). What wife wouldn't be built up and encouraged by a husband who loved her with the kind of sacrificial service Christ showed to His disciples? What child wouldn't be motivated and inspired to follow Christ after having seen Christ's love demonstrated and modeled by his or her father? On and on it goes. Our nurturing service to others at home, at church, or on the job, providing help, encouragement, and hope, will hopefully point others toward God and godly behavior.

This is quite a list, isn't it? Paul's comments about his brief time—a mere three weeks!—with the people of Thessalonica have given us nine great insights into what it means to have a heart for service. But given that Paul was with these people for such a short period of time, are you wondering whether Paul could possibly have had an effect on them?

Be sure and read the entire account for yourself in 1 Thessalonians 1:5-9. Here's a brief summary of the impact of Paul's heart for serving the Thessalonians:

They became converts.

They became imitators of Paul's life.

They became imitators of the Lord.

They became models to others.

They became messengers of the gospel to all.

Paul's influence was felt, even with such a short visit. Not only did Paul have an impact on these people, but these people, in turn, came to have an impact on others. Paul's influence was felt for hundreds of miles through the impact he made on this one group of people as they went about modeling Paul's heart for serving. Let's never be guilty of underestimating the power of a man with a servant's attitude!

Where to Start a Life of Servanthood

I hope that by now, you are seeing how you can influence others by having a servant's attitude, and that you are asking, "Where do I start?" Let me offer you a few tips on how to get started down the road to servanthood.

Servanthood is not natural—Start by praying that God would work in your heart. No man is the servant he *could* be. Ask God to make you the servant you should be.

Servanthood is not an office, but a ministry—Start by serving with humility. True influence always takes the posture of a servant.

Servanthood begins at home—Start by serving those who live under your own roof—your wife and children. What you are at home is what you are!

Servanthood is a lifestyle—Start by taking every opportunity to serve others at all times. A servant is not on part-time duty. He is fully committed in the whole of his being.

Servanthood has no selfish motives—Start by sacrificing your time, your money, and your energy for the needs of others. A servant gives, asking for nothing in return.

Servanthood is our calling—Start by acting like a servant. A servant is one who has been given a task by his Master. Own it!

Servanthood requires no training—Start today! No excuses can or should be given. What are you waiting for?

The Influence of a Servant

Serving others does have an influential effect on others. We saw this in the service of Jesus, D.L. Moody, and Paul, and in the two examples at the beginning of the previous chapter.

All through his life, one man selfishly took from others and basically had little or no impact. If he had any influence at all, it was negative.

On the other hand, my friend Stan Miller spent his whole life serving his family and anyone else who crossed his path. His godly influence was and will be felt for generations to come.

Now, my friend, which one of these men will you pattern your life after? Will you serve, or be served? The choice is yours. And remember...

*The greater the level of
your service to others,
the greater the level of
your influence on others.*

*The quality of your life will be determined by
the depth of your commitment to excellence,
no matter what your chosen field.*
—VINCE LOMBARDI

17

A Commitment to Excellence

*Whatever you do, whether in word or deed,
do it all in the name of the Lord Jesus.*

—Colossians 3:17

The captain of the plane came on the intercom with a cheery voice and announced that we were fifteenth in line to takeoff. Having put everything away in preparation for takeoff, Elizabeth and I sat in our plane seats with nothing to work on. If your job requires for you to fly, you know that's an unpardonable sin—plane time is work time!

So as we sat there on the runway at O'Hare Airport in Chicago, we began looking at the *Sky Mall* catalog that is placed in every seat pocket. (As you can tell, we were pretty desperate for something to do!) In the catalog we noticed a unique collection of audiotapes entitled "The World's 100 Greatest People." Can you imagine the honor it would be to end up on the list of the 100 greatest people out of the billions who have ever lived on this earth? *Who were these people,* we wondered, *and what made their influence so great? What had they done to become part of such an exclusive list?*

These questions were so compelling that I pulled out the telephone provided for plane passengers and made a collect call to order the tapes. As I hung up the phone, the captain came on the speaker and said we were making good progress...now there were only ten planes ahead of us!

Defining Excellence

With those questions continuing to bounce around in my head, the tapes finally arrived and I tore into the box and began to listen and learn about these people of influence—people with "Achieving Personalities," as they were described. I began to notice a single, shiny golden thread that was woven throughout the lives of these greats—every one of them had a commitment to excellence! Their lives of influence and accomplishment radiated a desire to do their best in their field of endeavor.

That's what excellence means—doing your best. Which brings us to our next visible sign of a man of influence—he, too, is committed to a life of excellence.

Many of the "world's 100 greatest people" were committed to excellence because they saw their life as a stewardship. And that should be our focus as well—which brings up another definition of excellence:

> Excellence is the maximum exercise of one's gifts and abilities within the range of responsibilities *given by God*.[38]

This is a very important definition, for it keeps in mind that God is the one who determines the standard of excellence for us. The measure of excellence is unique for each one of us because God has given each of us a different set of talents and abilities. And He expects you and me to be good stewards of those resources.

You and I must see our lives as a stewardship from God and an opportunity to fulfill His desires for our lives. How can we do this? Let me describe our stewardship as men of influence in this way—it's spelled E-X-C-E-L-L-E-N-C-E.

E - Eyes the goal—A man of influence lives a focused life. Regardless of the distractions that come his way, he concentrates on the matters that have the greatest importance. He knows and accepts that he will not be able to do all things, and certainly not do all things well. What one grand goal will your life be known for? Paul understood our need to keep our eyes on the goal. He declared, "This one thing I do," not "These many things I dabble in"!

X - Excels at finding solutions—A man of influence is creative. He is always thinking, always finding answers and fresh solutions. He is flexible, innovative, and always endeavors to find a way to make things work.

C - Curious about the future—A man of influence is a visionary. He is a forward thinker. He is a planner. He plans for the future in his personal life, in his business life, and ultimately he has planned for his future life in eternity. As a visionary, he will have a powerful and permanent influence on his generation because he is able to see more and farther ahead than others. He is a man of faith, for faith is vision.

E - Excited about change—A man of influence is flexible. He has a burning desire to know the truth and he is flexible, willing to make changes in his life if they're needed.

L - Learns from everyone—A man of influence has a passion for learning. He has an unquenchable thirst for growing, and he willingly seeks out anyone who can aid his thirst. He prepares himself for any task by researching, reading, and training. A man with a spirit of learning will encounter no hurdle he cannot overcome. It's been said that continuous learning is the minimum requirement for success in any field.

This passion for learning was a major element in the powerful influence of Henry Stanley, who lived in the 1800s and started his life with every disadvantage you could think of. He was deserted by his mother when he was only two and raised in a "poorhouse." Stanley could have excused himself (like most do!) from any opportunity to live a life of influence. Yet with a passion for learning, he went on to become a missionary and explorer in Africa, a member of the British parliament, and was knighted in 1899.

L - Loves to take risks—A man of influence is not a fool...but he is also not afraid to take risks. He simply will not settle for security and comfort. He is willing to break with convention if he believes that to be the will of God for his life. When I lived in Singapore with my family, I had the privilege of meeting Hudson Taylor, III, the great-grandson of Hudson Taylor, the founder of China Inland Mission. Hudson Taylor felt led by God to go to China. However, no mission board would sponsor him. So he founded China Inland Mission. Because of his willingness to take a risk, he and hundreds of others went to China under this mission's banner and were a great influence for the cause of Christ... all because God was able to use one man who was willing to take a risk.

E - Endures opposition—A man of influence is willing to endure pain, suffering, and persecution in order to accomplish God's demands on his life. He will persevere through all obstacles and opposition. We've already considered the apostle Paul's life of adversity—the prisons, the beatings, the treachery, the persecutions (2 Corinthians 11:23-27). "Yet," as is written, "from such rocky soil grew the fruit of his ministry. Adversity builds character, perspective and vision into the life of a leader." [39]

N - Names failure a learning experience—A man of influence has Resilience...with a capital R! He is able to bounce back after what seems to be a failure. He uses his failures as learning experiences. Every step is a step forward. And no defeat is final. Every time I think of this quality of excellence, I think of Thomas Edison, the great inventor of the light bulb, who endured 10,000 tries before he invented the incandescent lamp.

C - *Convinced of what he is doing*—A man of influence has conviction. Anything he believes to be the will of God is entered into with the full force of his being. Therefore he can endure great difficulty and adversity in the course of completing the task. His confidence is not in his own abilities, but in God's ability to work through his limited abilities. As martyred missionary Jim Elliot exhorted, "Live to the hilt any situation you believe to be the will of God."

E - *Envisions a higher purpose*—A man of influence has a sense of God's calling on his life. Whether he is a minister, a missionary, a mason, or a meter reader, he does his work as though doing it for the Lord (Colossians 3:23). He is compelled to live out every area of his life to the maximum (to the hilt!) for God's glory and the good of others.

Excellence. Brother, don't leave home without it! Endeavor, by God's grace, to live each day to its fullest, to live each day to its maximum, to live each day with excellence. And that, of course, is going to take commitment. As Vince Lombardi said in the quote at the beginning of this chapter, "The quality of your life will be determined by the depth of your commitment to excellence, no matter what your chosen field."

Determining to Become a Man of Excellence

The question for you (and me) today is this: Where, what, and how deep is your commitment to excellence? In relation to commitment, one sharp writer divided people into four types:

- *Cop-outs*—People who have no goals and do not make commitments.

- *Holdouts*—People who don't know if they can reach their goals, so they're afraid to make commitments.

- *Dropouts*—People who start toward a goal but quit when the going gets tough.

- *All-outs*—People who set goals, commit to them, and pay the price to reach them. [40]

I'm sure your desire is to do well with your commitments, to be an all-out man of influence who makes a lasting impact. With that desire in mind, here are some ways you can improve on making and keeping your commitments.

Determine the areas of your life where a greater commitment is needed—How you spend your time and money are the two greatest indicators of your focus and interest. So take a look at your calendar and your checkbook and determine what you've been committing yourself to. Ask yourself if these are the right priorities for you as a Christian man. Ask if these pursuits will enable you to have a lasting impact. Maybe you need to readjust your priorities. If you're a workaholic, a sports fanatic, or overly materialistic, maybe you need help in re-prioritizing your life. Remember to make the things of God your first priority. As the scripture verse for this chapter reminds us, "Whatever you do, whether in word or deed, do it all in the name of the Lord Jesus" (Colossians 3:17).

Determine the extent of commitment that is needed—Some areas of life call for more of a commitment than others. For instance, exercise requires commitment, but it doesn't demand the same level of commitment as your job. Ask God to help you discern the level of commitment required in each area of your life. And always remember that excellence ought to be your goal in all the areas you commit to. That's where the influence will come from!

Determine if you are willing to make that higher level of commitment—After giving thought and prayer to your priorities and the level of commitment needed in each area of your life, the next step is to determine if you are willing to pay the price of excellence. It will cost you to be a growing Christian man of influence. It will cost you to be a man of God. It will cost you to be the kind of husband the Bible calls you to be. It will cost you to be a good parent and to be the best at work. It will cost you to serve in your church. Commitment to excellence always comes at a cost!

Determine what it will take to keep your commitments—First, ask God to help you follow through on the commitments you want to make for His glory and the good of others. Second, ask someone to hold you accountable to those commitments. Finally, remember that God has handed you the baton for "the race of life." Others are depending on you to keep your commitments, whether it's at home, on the job, or at church. Please, don't drop the baton that's been passed to you...keep your commitments!

A Prayer to Pray

Lord, I want to thank You for Your commitment in securing my salvation in Jesus Christ.
I ask that You help me stay committed to the
standards of Your Word. Please give me wisdom as I determine my priorities. And I ask for
Your Holy Spirit to strengthen my resolve to
follow through on those priorities. May I
accept the challenge of a life committed to You.
From this day forward, as I seek to become a
man of influence, may I be known as one who
keeps his commitments, regardless of the cost.
Amen.

If I had my life to live over again,
I would live it to change the lives of people,
because you have not changed anything
until you've changed the lives of people.
—WARREN WEBSTER [41]

A Passion for Mentoring

The things you have heard me say
in the presence of many witnesses
entrust to reliable men
who will also be qualified to teach others.
—2 Timothy 2:2

The topic of mentoring has recently become very fashionable. Numerous books from both the business world and the church have been written on the subject of having and being a mentor.

Have you ever wondered where the concept of mentoring came from? I have…and I did a little research and discovered that the word *mentor* has an interesting history. It seems that in the eighth century B.C., the poet Homer wrote, in his major Greek work *The Odyssey*, about a man named *Mentor*. Mentor was the friend of the warrior Odysseus. When Odysseus went off to fight in the Trojan War, Mentor was left in charge of Odysseus's household. Mentor was also charged with teaching, tutoring, and protecting Odysseus's son, Telemachus. Mentor was faithful to "mentor" Telemachus until his father returned many years later.

This, my friend, is a great illustration of the meaning of the word *mentor*. In our culture today, anyone who is an experienced advisor, supporter, teacher, or tutor has taken on the title of *mentor* in the tradition of Odysseus's faithful friend, Mentor.

The Influence of a Mentor

With my busy schedule, I don't have a lot of time for hobbies. I do a little running and sometimes "pump a little iron." Beyond that I'm a pretty dull person. But one thing I enjoy doing is visiting the local bookstore wherever my business or ministry endeavors take me.

I prefer Christian bookstores for obvious reasons, but I also enjoy going into other bookstores. So whether it's one or the other, I delight in leafing through as many books as I can, looking for the right ones to purchase. My particular areas of interest are leadership, discipleship, mentoring, Bible studies, and Christian living. Over the years I have noticed a large number of books on the shelves that are dedicated to Dr. Howard Hendricks, professor of Christian Education at Dallas Theological Seminary.

Dr. Hendricks seems to epitomize what we want to cover in this chapter on becoming a man of influence— about having a passion for mentoring men. "Howie" (as many of his friends call him) has taught, trained, and influenced hundreds of men at the seminary where he has taught for more than 30 years. Howie's men have graduated and taken positions of influence all over the world. Over the years, these men have modeled their mentor and passed on to others what Dr. Hendricks passed on to them.

In fact, right now I am holding in my hand a book on excellence. And guess what? The forward was written by Howard D. Hendricks. This book in my hand, along with a myriad of other books and a myriad of men, speaks to the fact that Dr. Hendricks is living out the apostle Paul's exhortation to Timothy, his younger protégé, to train the generations to come—"the things you have heard me say in the presence of many witnesses entrust to reliable men who will also be qualified to teach others" (2 Timothy 2:2). Dr. Hendricks is living out that same exhortation for you and me as well.

The Example of a Good Mentor

Long before the word *mentor* became trendy, Paul, like Mentor, was a teacher and tutor. But, unlike Mentor, who trained only one young boy, Paul was an advisor and trainer of many. Paul supported, taught, and tutored a host of men and women during his 20-plus years of ministry. I believe Paul was able to utter the now-famous words at the end of his life—"I have finished the race"—partly because he passed on to others what had been given to him (2 Timothy 4:7). He told the leaders at Ephesus, "I have not hesitated to proclaim to you the whole will of God" (Acts 20:27). Paul held nothing back from anyone who cared to learn from him. He gave it all. He passed on all that he knew.

The Bible doesn't record how or when Paul's life ended. Maybe that's because, in a sense, Paul's life didn't end. The famous preacher John Wesley was often quoted as saying, "God buries His workmen, but His work goes on." Well, friend, God buried His servant Paul, but Paul's mentoring influence continued on through...

The young man Timothy—Timothy is probably the most well known of Paul's pupils. Paul had worked with Timothy for 15 years and, at the end of Paul's days on this earth, Timothy had matured and was pastoring the "flagship" church at Ephesus in Asia Minor. Paul's teaching would live on in the life and ministry of Timothy as Timothy fulfilled one of Paul's final exhortations to him: "The things you have heard me say in the presence of many witnesses entrust to reliable men who will also be qualified to teach others" (2 Timothy 2:2).

The young man Titus—Titus was another young man mentored by Paul. As with Timothy, Paul entrusted Titus with more and more responsibility as he matured in the faith. Because of his valuable mentoring, Paul's legacy and teaching would live on through the life and ministry of Titus.

The lives of others—Besides Timothy and Titus, there were a multitude of others who were deeply influenced by Paul. For instance...

- Paul had disciples from the very beginning of his ministry (in Damascus), and they helped him escape from his enemies (Acts 9:25). Paul's influence lived on in the lives of these faithful and fearless followers.

- Paul had disciples on his first missionary journey who were with him even in the midst of much persecution (Acts 14:19-20). In spite of difficult situations, Paul's influence lived on in the lives of these courageous disciples.

- Paul left disciples behind when he left Ephesus. In fact, the Ephesian elders evidenced their devotion to Paul by traveling over 40 hours to spend just a few hours with their beloved mentor as he passed nearby on his way to Jerusalem (Acts 20:17-18). When Paul left Ephesus, "he knelt down with all of them and prayed. They all wept as they embraced him and kissed him....Then they accompanied him to the ship" (Acts 20:36-38). Paul's influence would most definitely live on in the lives of these devoted men.

Talk about influence! And talk about the impact Paul had on the lives of other men! We can be sure their lives were never the same.

The Greatest Mentor of All

Now it's time to turn our attention to the discipleship and mentoring ministry of the greatest mentor of all, Jesus Christ. (That is another whole book in itself!) Without a doubt, Jesus was the greatest mentor of all times. He set the pattern for *everyone* to follow! He took a ragtag group of a dozen uneducated, ill-equipped men and, in three years, molded them into a force that turned the religious world of their day literally upside down. Now that's influence! How did He, the greatest mentor of all, do it?

1. Selection—Jesus prayerfully selected 12 men.

2. Association—Jesus spent time with His men.

3. Consecration—Jesus required obedience.

4. Impartation—Jesus gave Himself away, even His own life.

5. Demonstration—Jesus modeled godly living.

6. Delegation—Jesus assigned His disciples work to do.

7. Supervision—Jesus monitored the progress of His men.

8. Reproduction—Jesus expected His disciples to make disciples.[42]

Your Influence As a Mentor

As you can see from the lives of men like Paul and Howard Hendricks—and, of course, our Lord—significant influence and lasting impact requires an investment of time and concern for the lives of others. Again, you cannot have significant impact without significant contact. The closer you get to another person, the more influence you will have on that person's life.

So I must now ask the tough questions. Who are you getting close to? Who are you pouring your life into? Will you be able to say, "I have finished the race" because you have equipped others to carry on your philosophy, your life, your ministry, your influence? Are there others who have been so personally impacted by your life that long after you are gone, your ideals, principles, and vision will live on? These are difficult but important questions to ask. These are questions all of us need to ask before it's too late to have an impact on others.

Developing a Passion for Mentoring

When I arrived at the church where my family spent our first 30 years as a Christian family, I was a very immature believer. I didn't have a clue about what God was asking of me as a husband, father, provider, church member, or witness.

So what did I do to get the much-needed help? I began by looking around the church for men who were mature in the areas in which I was weak. Then I asked them to mentor me. Some of these men were younger than me, but that didn't matter! They were much farther along on the road to maturity than I was. They had what I needed!

As I matured in my faith and grew in my understanding of my roles, I began to sense the responsibility I had to pass on to others what I had been taught. As I grew, the passion to help others grew. Today, 30 years later, I receive about 10 to 20 emails, phone calls, or letters a week from men who tell me I have influenced their lives. When I say that, I'm not bragging! Far from it. I wish I could have given them more than I did. And I also wish I had awakened sooner to the opportunities I had for being a man of influence.

O man of God, start growing! And as you grow, God will give *you* the same passion men like Jesus, Paul, and Howard Hendricks have displayed for mentoring other men of God.

Then, as the title of the next chapter says, ours will be *an influence for life!*

God will one day bury you, His workman.
Your physical life will come to an end.
But your influence will not end.
God's workman will be gone,
but God's work will go on.
—JIM GEORGE

An Influence for Life

*Whatever you have learned or received or
heard from me, or seen in me—
put it into practice.*
—Philippians 4:9

On one of my visits to India, my friend Chris Williams, who is definitely a man of influence, took me to visit a retiring missionary. The missionary was in the midst of selling all of his equipment before he returned home. As we chatted, I asked the man, "Where are your men? Where are the men you've mentored and trained to take over your work now that you are retiring?"

Well, I must say I wasn't prepared for this older man's answer. There were none! He had no disciples. He had trained no one. This godly man and his family had sacrificed much over their 25 years of living and ministering in this severely impoverished country. Humanly speaking, all of that sacrifice would soon be visibly gone. Why? Because there were no disciples left behind to carry on the ministry. There would be no lasting influence through the lives of others.

Becoming Alert to Your Opportunities

What a wake-up call that was for me! And I hope it is to you as well. Brother, don't let your life slip away without personally and purposefully and positively influencing others. You have so much to give! And all through this book, you've learned how you can give—of yourself to God in obedience and discipline, of yourself in your own life and to others by setting the right goals, and of yourself to others by using your spiritual gifts and having a servant's heart. In all these ways, you can make sure that you leave a legacy to...

Your wife—If you are married, you have one of the greatest of all opportunities—that of leaving a lasting influence on the person who is the closest to you physically, emotionally, and spiritually, your wife. Make sure that before you die (keep in mind that insurance company statistics show that you will probably die before your wife does), you pass on a godly influence to your wife.

Dear brother, you must impart to your sweet and faithful wife a strong spiritual foundation so that she is better equipped to handle whatever the future holds. That means you must be a strong spiritual leader yourself. Don't leave behind only personal memories, as wonderful as they are. Memories fade with time. And don't leave behind only financial security. Money will take care of the physical needs, and that's important. But beyond these "things," seek to leave behind something greater—far greater! Leave behind a tower of spiritual strength that is being built now, today, through your godly example. Leave behind something that has true and lasting influence!

And yet, there is an even greater legacy than a wife who carries on your faith, your priorities, your principles, and your vision. There are...

Your children—Perhaps the greatest legacy you can leave behind is another godly generation. Humanly speaking, Christianity is only one generation away from extinction. Who will serve as a witness to the next generation? *You! You* are to pass on to your children the truth about Christ and Christian living. Your faith ought to become their faith. Now, we all know that we cannot grant salvation to our children. We cannot give them eternal life. No, that's God's job. But you and I can provide the right kind of godly influence in the home that will point our children to the Savior. The reality of Jesus Christ must first be evident in your life and my life before we can point our children to that same reality.

Now, I must warn you, if you haven't already found this out, your children may resist your Christian focus. They may object to your Christian standards. They may complain of your direction for their lives. But don't give in. There is a war going on for their souls and for their purity, just as there is a war going on for your soul and your purity. Do your part to provide a godly influence, and trust God to do the rest.

Your fellow Christians—Maybe you are reading this book and you don't have a family. Well, my friend, we all have an opportunity to influence our fellow believers, both now and in the future. Like Paul and like Timothy and Titus, you have the opportunity to spend your life mentoring others. You can make 2 Timothy 2:2 one of your life verses: "The things you have heard me say...entrust to reliable men who will also be qualified to teach others."

Whether or not we have a family, we are all called to mentor other believers at church. We are to actively look for those whom we can bring along in the faith. We, like Paul, need to be about the business of coming alongside a Timothy or a Titus and overseeing their growth in maturity and watching them flourish in their usefulness to the church. How, you ask, can you be this kind of mentor in your church?

- First, (as I've said before) you must be growing in your own faith. You cannot impart to others what you do not possess yourself.

- Second, understand and develop your spiritual gifts. As we learned earlier, God has given you special spiritual abilities for the purpose of serving others and building up your local church. Reading and studying what the Bible says about spiritual gifts will help you get a grasp of these important God-given tools (see Romans 12:4-8; 1 Corinthians 12:1-31; 1 Peter 4:10-11). With God's gifts, you can impact the lives of other Christians! Don't neglect to discover, develop, and use your gifts.

- Third, look for men who want to grow in their faith. I have often heard it put this way: "Look for *fat* men." This is not a reference to waist size. No, it's talking about...

F - aithfulness—Look for faithful men. Look for men who are where they are supposed to be, when they are supposed to be there. Look for men you can count on to do what they say they will do. Faithfulness is difficult to find, but it is an indispensable quality.

A - vailable—Look for men who are available. Look for men who are willing to give of their time in order to be trained and equipped for life and ministry. God is not looking solely for ability—He is looking for availability! And so should you.

T - eachable—Look for teachable men. Look for men who want to learn...and more specifically, men who want to learn from you. You might be thinking, *But...what can I offer to another man? What do I have that another man might benefit from?* Well, for one thing, you have read this book. You now know more than someone else knows. There are study questions in the back of the book, so take another man through this book and discuss the questions as you go through it together. Find other men and teach them what you know.

And there is yet another area where your influence is needed...

Your world—Many people in your life have little or no contact with a Christian other than you. They may see a "Christian" on TV or read about Christians in the paper (usually in a negative light), or watch them in their neighborhood going off to church in their Sunday best. But they will seldom actually meet one up close and personal other than you. It's been said in a poem that "you are a living Bible, known and read by men." The clever rhyme goes on to ask, "What does the Bible say, 'according to you'?"

So, what kind of influence are you in your neighborhood? Are you exhibiting a proper representation of Christianity? And how about your behavior at work? Are you kind, thoughtful, friendly? Are you willing to help others succeed, even at your own expense? Are you going about the business of mentoring others on the job to help make your company more effective and productive? How are your relationships with your subordinates? Are you developing them, or are you using them? Just what does the Bible say, according to you?

Leaving a Lasting Legacy

Well, my friend, we have come a long way in learning about how to become God's man of influence. We've learned from the lives of Christ Himself, the Master Discipler...the apostle Paul...the influential Howard Hendricks...and others. And now, the baton is being passed on to you. Do you want to have a lasting influence? I'm sure that like me, you want your life to be marked by positive, solid, biblical, and Christ-honoring qualities that can be passed on to others. If so, then here are some suggestions on how your influence can be felt now and for generations to come.

- Be a consistent, godly example. Start in your home.

- Be growing in your faith. God is not asking for perfection—just progression. Grow toward maturity, and pass on to others what you learn.

- Be growing in your job skills. God is asking you to work as if you were working for Him (Colossians 3:23).

- Be aware of your influence on others. Make sure it is a positive influence.

- Be available. Whether at home, at church, or on the job, others need your personal involvement in their lives.

- Be mentoring. Not only should you be available, but you should be actively training others.

- Be faithful, and then you will...

- Be fulfilled!

Dear friend, God will one day bury you, His workman, just as He buried his servant and workman Paul. Your physical life will come to an end. But your influence will not end. No, as you are faithful to pour your life into your family, your friends, your fellow workmates, and into fellow believers at church, your influence will live on through the lives of those whom you have served during your life. God's workman will be gone, but God's work will go on. You, His messenger and mentor, will be gone, but God's message will continue on. May your life and influence live on. May yours be a life of lasting impact.

Live on, my friend. Live on!

Study Questions for Becoming a Man of Influence

Part 1: *The Secrets of a Life of Influence*

Chapter 1—Profiling a Man of Influence

1. Read again the profile of the apostle Paul on pages 12-13. Jot down three areas of your life in which you believe you are making good progress. Then make a note of three areas you know require your attention.

2. Think about Paul's appearance, his age, and the adversities he suffered. Can you relate to any of them? How does Paul's dedication encourage you to get into the race, stay in the race, and keep on keeping on?

3. What one truth from this chapter had the greatest impact on you, and why? After you identify the "one truth" from this chapter, record it on the "One Truth List" at the back of your book on pages 198-99.

Chapter 2— Taking the First Step Toward Influence
1. Briefly describe your own dramatic encounter with the Master.

2. Read again the lists of "before and after" truths about a man's life before Christ (page 23) and after Christ (pages 24-25). How do these truths encourage you and/or humble you?

3. What one truth from this chapter had the greatest impact on you, and why? Write this on the "One Truth List" on pages 198-99.

Chapter 3—Living a Life of Obedience

1. What did you like about the man Ananias? How does his life "influence" yours?

2. What impresses you the most about these men of influence—Abraham, Moses, and Daniel? How do they encourage you in your obedience?

3. What one truth from this chapter had the greatest impact on you, and why? Add this to your "One Truth List."

Chapter 4—Following the Path of Obedience

1. Review how the path of obedience leads you to the unexpected, to clarification, and to confidence as you listen and make one decision at a time. What hit your heart the hardest, and why?

2. Name a decision you must make. How do you think "the four C's" can help you, and how will you put them to use in making your decision?

3. What one truth from this chapter had the greatest impact on you, and why? Add this to your list.

Chapter 5—Mastering Life's Challenges
1. Skim through this chapter again and list the challenges or hurdles that can trip up a man's obedience. Mark the one that bothers you the most.

2. Ask and answer the questions on page 53, which is designed to help you check your spiritual temperature. What spiritual prescription can you apply today (pages 53-54)?

3. What one truth from this chapter had the greatest impact on you, and why? It goes without saying...add this to your list!

Chapter 6—Accepting the Challenge to Live Boldly
1. Skim through this chapter, and continue listing the challenges and hurdles to obedience. Again, mark the one that bothers you the most.

2. Jot down the five simple steps for living a strong, bold life of influence. Which step will you take today?

3. What one truth from this chapter had the greatest impact on you, and why?

Chapter 7—Pursuing Spiritual Discipline
1. Think of an athlete you admire. In what ways are that person and the apostle Paul alike, and in what ways do they differ?

2. In your Bible, read the latter portion of 1 Timothy 4:7 and write it here and commit it to memory. Then list the three characteristics of spiritual discipline presented in this chapter. How can you pursue spiritual discipline more intently, like an athlete who pursues a prize?

3. What one truth from this chapter had the greatest impact on you, and why?

Chapter 8—Practicing Personal Discipline

1. This chapter mentions the five steps toward a more disciplined life. List those steps here.

2. If it's true every journey begins with a single step, what first step will you take to better practice personal discipline...and when?

3. Read again page 84, entitled "The Nature of Discipline." Mark three items that would most cause your life to be more disciplined. What will you do about them...and when?

4. What one truth from this chapter had the greatest impact on you, and why? (Remember to keep up your "One Truth List.")

Chapter 9—Developing Lifelong Goals

1. Yes...or no—have you written down any of your life goals? If so, review them now. If not, stop, get your calendar, and schedule a time to develop your lifetime goals—then write them down.

2. Scan through the benefits of having goals (pages 89-91). Then measure the spiritual and mental areas of your life. How can you improve and develop these two major areas of your life?

3. What one truth from this chapter had the greatest impact on you, and why?

Chapter 10—Defining Your Purpose

1. Take a moment to review how you've improved in the spiritual and mental areas of your life last week (in response to the second question for chapter 9).

2. Going back to chapter 9 in the book, scan again the benefits of having goals. Then measure the physical, social, and vocational areas of your life. How can you improve and develop these three major areas of your life?

3. What one truth from this chapter had the greatest impact on you, and why?

Chapter 11—Practicing God's Plan
1. Take a moment to note how you've improved in the physical, social, and vocational areas of your life.

2. Going back to chapter 9, scan again the benefits of having goals. Then measure the financial, family, and ministry areas of your life. How can you improve and develop these three major areas of your life?

3. What one truth from this chapter had the greatest impact on you, and why?

Chapter 12—Dealing with Temptation

1. Read again the section "Two Men, Two Choices, Two Paths." How do these two scenarios describe any of the struggles and paths you have faced in your life?

2. What encouragement can you draw from the four provisions God has supplied for you in dealing with your temptations? Is there any one provision in particular you need to use today?

3. What one truth from this chapter had the greatest impact on you, and why?

Chapter 13—Fighting the Battle Against Temptation

1. Life is a battle! Do you agree or disagree? What happens to the man who fails to recognize life is a battle? What does Ephesians 6:10-18 say about how you can prepare to fight, the inevitable battle, and experience victory?

2. Review the three types of temptation discussed in this chapter. Which one do you face most in your daily life? What suggestions did you find that will help you fight your battles against temptation? Can you think of other suggestions?

3. What one truth from this chapter had the greatest impact on you, and why?

Chapter 14—Looking at Your Secret Life
1. In the first 14 chapters of this book, we focused on *the secrets of a life of influence.* Make an abbreviated list of the eight indicators of progress in a maturing man's spiritual life. Are there any weak areas you must shore up? Share briefly what you will do about this.

2. Of the two images—an awesome iceberg and a majestic mountain—which do you like best as an illustration of a man of influence? Now, does this accurately describe *your* life? Why or why not?

3. What one truth from this chapter had the greatest impact on you, and why?

Part 2: *The Signs of a Life of Influence*

Chapter 15—A Heart for Serving

1. In this chapter, we began looking at nine insights on becoming a servant. Write the first two from this chapter. In regard to Insight #1, do you consider yourself to be serving for a higher purpose?

2. As you think about Insight #2, describe your present situation in a very few words. Are you allowing this situation—or anything else—to keep you from serving God and His people? How does the quote from missionary T.J. Bach help you in your situation?

3. What one truth from this chapter had the greatest impact on you, and why? (Be sure to keep up your "One Truth List" throughout this section of your study.)

Chapter 16—An Attitude of Servanthood

1. Read again 1 Thessalonians 2:1-12 and review your notes from the previous chapter, noting the first two insights into an attitude of servanthood. Add the seven additional insights from this chapter to your list. Mark the insight that meant the most to you and share why.

2. List now the qualities of servanthood. What will you do to either get started or to "turn up the heat" on your service?

3. What one truth from this chapter had the greatest impact on you, and why?

Chapter 17—A Commitment to Excellence

1. Jot down the acrostic for E-X-C-E-L-L-E-N-C-E. It's a lot to think and pray about! In which area are you the strongest, and in which are you the weakest? Why did you choose these two?

2. Now list the four "determinations" that can deepen your commitment to excellence. Which "determination" are you planning to act on immediately? What will you do?

3. What one truth from this chapter had the greatest impact on you, and why?

Chapter 18—A Passion for Mentoring

1. Think of a man who influenced your life by mentoring you, whether by model or by mouth. What are two lessons he passed on to you?

2. Review Jesus' mentoring ministry, and Paul's as well. What stands out the most from each man's passion for training others?

3. What one truth from this chapter had the greatest impact on you, and why?

Chapter 19—An Influence for Life

1. Spend a few minutes thinking about your influence on your wife, your children, your fellow Christians, and your world. Are you taking steps to have a lasting influence in their lives? What must you do or change to ensure that your life and influence "live on"?

2. Are you a *F-A-T* man (see page 182)? Explain how you're doing in all three areas. Once again, are there any changes you need to make?

3. What one truth from this chapter had the greatest impact on you, and why?

4. *Bonus Question*—Review the "One Truth List" on pages 198-99. Record the most serious change you have made during this study, in...

   ...your personal life—

...your home life—

...your public life—

Then take time to thank God that you are well on the road to becoming a man of influence, a man who leaves a lasting impact on others.

Live on, my friend, live on!

One Truth List

Chapter	Truth That Had the Greatest Impact
1.	
2.	
3.	
4.	
5.	
6.	
7.	
8.	
9.	

10.

_____

11.

_____

12.

_____

13.

_____

14.

_____

15.

_____

16.

_____

17.

_____

18.

_____

19.

_____

NOTES

1. Eleanor L. Doan, *The Speaker's Sourcebook* (Grand Rapids, MI: Zondervan Publishing House, 1977), p. 133.

2. John F. Kennedy, *Profiles in Courage*, inaugural edition (New York: Harper and Row, 1955).

3. John Pollock, *The Man Who Shook the World* (Wheaton, IL: Victor Books, 1973), p. 39.

4. Merrill C. Tenney, gen. ed., *The Zondervan Pictorial Encyclopedia of the Bible*, vol. 4 (Grand Rapids, MI: Zondervan Publishing House, 1975), p. 625.

5. D.A. Hayes, *Paul and His Epistles* (Grand Rapids: Baker Book House, 1968).

6. Pollock, *The Man Who Shook the World*

7. As cited in *World Shapers* (Wheaton, IL: Harold Shaw Publishers, 1991), p. 16.

8. Doan, *The Speaker's Sourcebook*, quoting Cal Stargel, "In This Day," p. 133.

9. Charles R. Swindoll, *Paul: A Man of Grace and Grit* (Nashville, TN: W Publishing Group, 2002), p. 17.

10. Hymn "Hallelujah, What a Savior!" by Phillip P. Bliss.

11. "I Met the Master Face to Face," author/source unknown.

12. As cited in *World Shapers* (Wheaton, IL: Harold Shaw Publishers, 1991), p. 90.

13. Kenneth W. Osbeck, *Amazing Grace* (Grand Rapids, MI: Kregel Publications, 1990), p. 88.

14. Roy B. Zuck, *The Speaker's Quote Book* (Grand Rapids, MI: Kregel Publications, 1997), p. 16.

15. Romans 11:25; 1 Corinthians 12:1; 2 Corinthians 1:8; 1 Thessalonians 4:13 NKJV.

16. Zuck, *The Speaker's Quote Book*, p. 38.

17. John Witherspoon as cited in Albert M. Wells, Jr., *Inspiring Quotations—Contemporary and Classical* (Nashville, TN: Thomas Nelson Publishers, 1988), p. 73.

18. R. Kent Hughes, *Disciplines of a Godly Man* (Wheaton, IL: Crossway Books, 1991), p. 15.

19. John F. MacArthur, *The MacArthur New Testament Commentary–1 Timothy* (Chicago, IL: Moody Press, 1995), p. 164.

20. Ibid.

21. Oswald Chambers as cited in Wells, *Inspiring Quotations*, p. 73.

22. Richard S. Taylor, *The Disciplined Life* (Minneapolis, MN: Bethany House Publishers, 1962), p. 23.

23. V. Raymond Edman, *The Disciplines of Life* (Minneapolis, MN: World Wide Publications, 1948), p. 9.

24. Taylor, *The Disciplined Life*, p. 23.

25. Edward R. Dayton and Ted W. Engstrom, *Strategy for Living* (Glendale, CA: Regal Books Division G/L Publications, 1978), p. 32.

26. A.B. Simpson as cited in Wells, *Inspiring Quotations*, p. 73.

27. Hughes, *Disciplines of a Godly Man*, pp. 62-63.

28. Sherwood Eliot Wirt and Kersten Beckstrom, quoting Henry R. Brandt, *Topical Encyclopedia of Living Quotations* (Minneapolis, MN: Bethany House Publishers, 1982), p. 86.

29. Stephen Arterburn and Fred Stoeker, *Every Man's Battle* (Colorado Springs, CO: WaterBrook Press, 2000), p. 4.

30. Charles R. Swindoll, *The Quest for Character* (Portland, OR: Multnomah Press, 1987), p. 21.

31. Wells, *Inspiring Quotations*, p. 128.

32. D.L. Moody, *Notes from My Bible and Thoughts from My Library*, quoting Pushon (Grand Rapids, MI: Baker Book House, 1979), p. 331.

33. *Checklist for Life for Men*, quoting Douglas Groothuis (Nashville, TN: Thomas Nelson Publishers, 2002), p. 135.

34. As cited in *World Shapers*, p. 121.

35. Ibid., p. 75.

36. John C. Maxwell, *The 21 Indispensable Qualities of a Leader* (Nashville, TN: Thomas Nelson Publishers, 1999), pp. 135-36.

37. Jim George, *God's Wisdom for Little Boys* (Eugene, OR: Harvest House Publishers, 2002).

38. Gary Inrig, *A Call to Excellence* (Wheaton, IL: Victor Books, 1985), p. 87.

39. Sid Buzzell, gen. ed., *The Leadership Bible* (Grand Rapids, MI: Zondervan Publishing House, 1998), p. 1366.

40. Maxwell, *The 21 Indispensable Qualities of a Leader*, p. 20.

41. Charles R. Swindoll, *The Tale of the Tardy Oxcart*, quoting Warren Webster (Nashville, TN: Word Publishing, 1998), p. 300.

42. Robert E. Coleman, *The Master Plan of Evangelism* (Old Tappan, NJ: Fleming H. Revell Company, 1987), p. 7.

Personal Notes

Personal Notes

An Invitation to Write

Jim George is a teacher and speaker and the author of *A Man After God's Own Heart*. If you would like to receive more information about other books and audiotapes by Jim George, or if you want to share how *God's Man of* ™ *Influence* has influenced your life, you can write to him at:

Jim George
P.O. Box 2879
Belfair, WA 98528
Toll-free fax/phone: 1-800-542-4611
www.jimgeorge.com

Other Harvest House Books
by Jim George

A Man After God's Own Heart

Many Christian men want to be men after God's own heart...but how do they do this? George shows that a heartfelt desire to grow spiritually is all that's needed. God's grace does the rest.

God's Wisdom for Little Boys—Character-Building Fun from Proverbs (co-authored with Elizabeth George)

Share with the little boy in your life the gift of God's wisdom from Proverbs, and celebrate with him the character and traits of a godly man. As you read together fun rhymes that illustrate wisdom and strength, he will discover how special he is as a child of God.